ROOT

**A
MEMPHIS
HOOPS DREAM**

ROOT

A
MEMPHIS
HOOPS DREAM

**FOREWORD BY
HALL OF FAME COACH**

JOHN CALIPARI

Copyright © 2025 NATHANIEL ROOT
Two Penny Publishing
1209 SE 21st Avenue
Cape Coral, FL 33990

TwoPennyPublishing.com
info@twopennypublishing.com

All rights reserved. No part of this publication may be reproduced, distributed, or transmitted in any form or by any means, including photocopying, recording, or other electronic or mechanical methods, without the prior written permission of the publisher, except by a reviewer who wishes to quote brief passages in connection with a review written for inclusion in a magazine, newspaper, website, or broadcast.

ISBN: 978-1-965341-20-9
eBook also available

For information about this author, to book an event appearance, or a media interview, please contact the author.

FIRST EDITION

Two Penny Publishing is a partnership publisher of a variety of genres. We help first-time and seasoned authors share their stories, passion, knowledge, and experiences that help others grow and learn. Please visit our website, TwoPennyPublishing.com if you would like us to consider your manuscript or book idea for publishing.

Dedication

For my mother, Nona Plunk Root (1943–2017), lovingly known as Momma Root—

Your unwavering love, strength, and sacrifice gave me my roots.
You believed in me long before the world ever knew my name.
Every step I took on the hardwood, every moment I pushed through,
I carried your voice, your faith, and your spirit with me.
This dream was watered by your prayers.
I wish you were here to read it, but this book is for you.

CONTENTS

Foreword: By John Calipari ix
Chapter 1: Game Day: The Manifestation of a Dream 1
Chapter 2: Hard Lessons and Hay Fields 7
Chapter 3: The Root Mentality 11
Chapter 4: Voices of My Foundation 15
Chapter 5: Lessons from the Legends 19
Chapter 6: The Start of a Powerhouse 23
Chapter 7: Foundations of Determination 27
Chapter 8: Strength Through Adversity 33
Chapter 9: The Road to 32 37
Chapter 10: Bonds Built, Brick by Brick 41
Chapter 11: Confronting the Unexpected 47
Chapter 12: Against the Clock: Rising Through the Challenge 51
Chapter 13: Moments That Shape a Legacy 55
Chapter 14: The Road to Memphis 59
Chapter 15: Welcome to the Jungle 65
Chapter 16: Dealing with the Disappointment 69
Chapter 17: The Start of Something Big 83
Chapter 18: The News 87
Chapter 19: Back to the Beginning 93
Chapter 20: Milestones and Moments 97
Chapter 21: The Arrival 101
Chapter 22: From the Finch Center to the Pyramid 107
Chapter 23: Earning My Stripes 111
Chapter 24: The Streak 115
Chapter 25: No Excuses 119
Chapter 26: Earned, Not Given 123
Chapter 27: Falling Short, Aiming High 129
Chapter 28: Big Moments, Bigger Lessons 133
Chapter 29: Bringing It Home 139
Chapter 30: Resilience Over Regret 143
Chapter 31: Moments That Define Us 147
Chapter 32: The Final Chapter 151
Epilogue 155
Acknowledgments 161
About the Author 165

FOREWORD

When I think about the kind of player every coach hopes to have in their program, Root immediately comes to mind. He didn't come to Memphis with a five-star ranking or national media attention. What he brought was something far more valuable—an unwavering work ethic, a relentless drive to improve, and a desire to show that he belonged.

Root was the ultimate walk-on. He showed up early, stayed late, and was always willing to sacrifice and do whatever extra was needed to help the team. He just wanted to be part of something bigger than himself, and he earned that right every single day. Whether it was pushing scholarship players in practice, setting the tone in the weight room, or diving for loose balls when no one else would, he gave us everything he had. And when you have someone like that in your program, it becomes contagious. His presence raised the standard for everyone. That's exactly why he earned a scholarship—because he didn't just fill a roster spot, he elevated the entire team.

Coaching Root wasn't about drawing up plays for him or putting the ball in his hands. It was about watching a young man embody the spirit of the team, the soul of Memphis. He bought into every aspect of what we were trying to build—not just with his actions, but with his heart. And the beautiful part was, the city of Memphis saw that. The fans embraced him, not because he scored the most points, but because they recognized something real: a kid who never quit, who stayed grounded, and who represented their grit, toughness, and pride.

I've coached NBA All-Stars and first-round picks, but I'll always remember Root because he reminded all of us what it means to love the game and appreciate every opportunity it gives you. This book is more than a basketball story—it's a testament to belief, perseverance, and purpose. And if you're lucky, it just might light a fire in you, too.

—Coach John Calipari, Head Men's Basketball Coach at the University of Arkansas

CHAPTER 1

Game Day: The Manifestation of a Dream

"Success is not the destination, it's the journey."
ARTHUR ASHE

February 5, 2000

I woke up in my Marriott hotel room in downtown Memphis, Tennessee, staring at the ceiling, barely having slept a wink. It didn't matter how comfortable the bed was—I'd been tossing and turning all night, my mind racing with thoughts of what was ahead. This wasn't just another day. Even though the season was more than halfway over, for me, it felt like everything was just beginning. This was THE day—my first game as a Memphis Tiger.

As the early morning light crept in through the hotel curtains, I finally got up. I pulled them open, revealing a stunning view of the Pyramid Arena, its massive structure towering solemnly over the banks of the Mississippi River. The sight was both awe-inspiring and intimidating, reminding me that today was no ordinary day.

Eager to start the day, I headed down to one of the hotel's grand ballrooms where a breakfast buffet was laid out for the team. The atmosphere among my new teammates was a mixture of nervous energy and camaraderie, for tonight, we played our heated rivals... Louisville, led by Hall of Fame Coach Denny Crum. We exchanged jokes and predictions for the game, trying to keep the mood light, but the underlying tension was felt. It was more than just a meal; it was a shared ritual of preparation and focus.

After breakfast, we were given some time to ourselves. I returned to my room, staring back out at the Pyramid, feeling that same combination of nerves and excitement swirling in my stomach. Every minute seemed to crawl by.

Around midday, we finally loaded up our charter bus and headed over to the Pyramid for a shootaround. Everyone had their headphones on—CD players and Walkmans in their laps—locked in, visualizing the game ahead. The shootaround was crucial, not just for warming up our bodies but also for settling our minds. As I took my shots, each swoosh through the net built my confidence, readying me for the evening when the stands would be filled and all eyes would be on us.

Afterward, we headed back to the Memphis campus for some downtime before having to report back to the arena for the game. We only stayed in the hotel the night before the games so the coaches could keep an eye on us and make sure everyone stayed locked in—no distractions, no excuses.

Fellow freshman, and our 7-foot center, Earl Barron and I had already decided we'd ride back together early, about thirty minutes ahead of the rest of the team. Neither one of us wanted to be late or miss a second of soaking in that atmosphere.

Back in my dorm room, I lay down for a quick power nap. I closed my eyes for what felt like a heartbeat before my alarm jolted me awake. It was go-time.

Earl met me at my truck, his towering frame folding into the passenger seat. We popped in our favorite 3-6 Mafia CD, the beats filling the truck as we headed downtown. Driving down North Parkway and crossing over Danny Thomas Blvd., the Pyramid suddenly came into view. It rose majestically from the delta, its glass exterior catching the late afternoon sun in a spectacular display of light and reflections. It was a sight that took my breath away, a reminder of the grandeur of the moment and the game that awaited us.

As we pulled up to the guard booth at the arena, the security team immediately recognized us and waved us through into the parking lot. They directed us around to the back of the arena to the players-only entrance, an exclusive gateway that made the experience even more surreal.

Walking through the lower level beneath the arena, the event workers greeted us with enthusiastic high-fives and chants of "Let's Go Tigers!" Each shout and cheer built our excitement and anticipation, a surge of support that propelled us towards the locker room.

It was electric!

We walked through the tunnel and into the foyer outside the locker room. The big Memphis logo glowed on the wall like a spotlight welcoming us home. And when I stepped through the next door into the locker room, there it was—my jersey.

Number 4. "Root" stitched across the back.

I just stood there staring at it. I did wish that jersey had my cherished number 32 on it, but honestly, I would've worn any number just to be out there.

That jersey wasn't just fabric. It was the embodiment of every dream I'd ever chased. It was every early morning, every late-night gym session, every ounce of sweat, sacrifice, and self-belief, and it was for every person who overlooked me, doubted me, or told me this dream was out of my reach.

I bowed my head right there in front of my jersey, said a prayer, and thanked God for letting me live this dream.

After being taped by our trainer, Ray Burr, I went back to my locker and started getting dressed—jersey, shoes, and warm-ups. Each piece felt like armor, fortifying me for the battle ahead. Before I put on my shoes, I noticed that many of the players had written something inspirational on their shoes. I had so many people to be thankful for and who had inspired me to get to this point, but there could only be one thing I could write on my shoes. I quickly grabbed a Sharpie from one of the managers and carefully wrote the Roman numeral "III" on them, honoring my brother, George Root III. It was a simple yet powerful reminder of the support and inspiration that had carried me to this moment.

As we made our way out onto the court for warm-ups, the crowd was already buzzing. The arena wasn't full yet, but my eyes immediately found my family—my parents, Uncle Ned, and Grandmother Dean—sitting right where I'd left their tickets. I also caught a glimpse of some familiar faces in the student section—my fraternity brothers from Sigma Phi Epsilon, already leading the "ROOOTTT" chants. I couldn't help but smile.

Despite it being my first game, the familiarity of the cheers, the faces in the crowd, and the routine pre-game preparations made me feel like I had been part of the team for an entire season. The connection was instantaneous. As I warmed up, dribbling and taking shots, every nerve felt alive with the realization that this was it—my moment as a Memphis Tiger.

After warm-ups, we filed back into the locker room for final instructions. Coach Johnny Jones, our head coach, entered our meeting room. His presence commanded attention, and as he began to speak, his words were both riveting and motivating. He talked about family, toughness, and representing the city of Memphis every time we put on that jersey.

Then it was time.

As we got ready to run out for player introductions, Keiron Shine turned to me and said, "Shortest to tallest, Root. That means you're leading us out."

I laughed. At six feet tall, I wasn't accustomed to being called the shortest, but the scales were different in college basketball. Yet here I was, about to lead the Memphis Tigers out for my first game.

The entrance was nothing short of cinematic. We lined up behind the massive inflatable tiger head, the cheerleaders waving their tiger flags in front as smoke billowed around us, creating an almost mystical atmosphere. The roar of the crowd reached a deafening level as we burst through the tunnel. I led the charge, running beneath the towering tiger, feeling a rush like no other.

This was everything I had ever dreamed of—and then some. The energy of the crowd, the intensity of the moment, and the thrill of

GAME DAY: THE MANIFESTATION OF A DREAM

leading the team out welded into a singular, unforgettable experience of my first game as a Memphis Tiger.

As we lined up for intros, Louisville's starting five were introduced to a chorus of boos that only Memphis fans can deliver.

Then, the arena lights snapped off, plunging the space into darkness and instantly ramping up the atmosphere. A moment later, the hype video erupted on the jumbotron, a montage of season highlights, the crowd's cheers growing louder with each play displayed. The excitement was electrifying, a pulsating force that seemed to vibrate through the arena.

The place was rocking.

Then, it was our turn.

The opening chords of "Eye of the Tiger" blasted through the speakers, the iconic anthem syncing perfectly with the sudden eruption of fireworks and flames shooting up from behind the backboards. The crowd was frenzied now, their roars nearly deafening. The announcer let the song build to a crescendo before launching into the starting lineup announcements, his voice booming over the PA system.

The starters were introduced one by one; the crowd erupted louder with each name. The energy was off the charts. Finding a place on the bench, I tried to soak in every detail of the scene unfolding before me. The energy of the arena, the intensity of the fans, the anticipation of the tip-off—it was all more exhilarating than I could have imagined.

The game itself was a battle.

Louisville came in hot, jumping out to an 11–0 lead before Kelly Wise finally got us on the board. But we fought back. We clawed and scraped our way to within 9 points by halftime.

In the locker room, Coach Jones, recognizing the need for a shift in momentum, delivered a fiery and impassioned halftime speech, challenging us to respond.

And we did.

Kelly Wise scored 8 straight points to start the second half, cutting Louisville's lead to 1. But Louisville punched back, eventually pulling away late.

ROOT

As the final minutes ticked away and the outcome was all but decided, a low murmur began to ripple through the crowd. I started to hear something faint…and then louder…and louder still…

"ROOOTTT!"

Sixteen thousand fans chanting my name.

The chant captured Coach Jones's attention. He glanced down the bench, locked eyes with me, and said, "Root! Get in!"

My heart raced. This was the moment I had dreamed of—the culmination of years of dedication and hard work. With a mix of nerves and excitement, I shed my warmups.

As the horn sounded, the referee motioned me onto the court. I stepped onto the floor, my first official play as a Memphis Tiger about to unfold. I had done it; I was no longer just a spectator or a hopeful benchwarmer—I was a player in the game, my lifelong dream unfolding in real time.

CHAPTER 2

Hard Lessons and Hay Fields

"Character is formed not in comfort, but in the grind of ordinary days."
ANN HOWARD CREEL

I was born in the quiet, rural expanse of McNairy County, Tennessee, on 200 acres of rolling land we lovingly called "The Plunkerosa" or simply "The Farm." Named after my mother's family—the Plunks—this land shaped who I would become. With woods, a creek, and no neighbors in sight, it was the perfect backdrop for childhood adventures.

My parents, George Jr. and Nona (Plunk) Root, were originally from Memphis, Tennessee. Dad was a bricklayer and owner of Root Masonry, but his claim to fame was setting a land speed record on a motorcycle at Bonneville in 1972. Mom was a schoolteacher and an athlete. She made history as a member of Memphis State's first women's volleyball team under Elma Roane, the legendary coach whose name still graces the university fieldhouse.

I grew up with two siblings—my older brother, George III, and my twin sister, Natalie. George, whom I admired and looked up to, was just 18 months older, and even though I tried to compete, he always seemed a step ahead. He excelled in band, basketball, running, and several other activities. He is the hardest-working, strongest-minded, and most dedicated person I have ever met. Hence, the reason I took a Sharpie and wrote the Roman numeral "III" on my basketball shoes.

Natalie and I were born 24 minutes apart—a gap she never let me forget. Our parents didn't even know they were having twins until seven months into the pregnancy. Natalie was quiet but fierce. She tried every sport, stuck with soccer, and always dragged me into games and make-believe until we were old enough to go our separate ways athletically. But our bond as twins always held strong.

We were raised Catholic, and Mass was a non-negotiable part of our lives. Our Catholic faith was the backbone of our upbringing, instilling strong values and a deep sense of faith in us. We learned about sacraments, Scripture, humility, and service—not just in theory, but in practice. Our church taught us values that anchored our family, and they're still with me today.

Our expansive land became a playground for countless adventures, fostering a deep bond between us. Our parents instilled in us the values of hard work, perseverance, and the importance of chasing our dreams, no matter how unconventional. Our farm was more than land—it was a world of imagination. Our childhood was filled with the freedom to roam and discover, fostering a sense of adventure and curiosity. We spent hours hunting, exploring, and inventing games in the woods. One hill covered in exposed roots was our favorite place. We called it Snake Mountain. We'd climb and crawl all over it, as if it were our private jungle gym. Every twist of a root was a new path or challenge. It wasn't just a hill. It was a place where we tested our limits, created stories, and forged unforgettable childhood memories.

Nights during basketball season, I would lie sprawled out on the living room floor, the worn carpet beneath me. We'd tune in to Memphis basketball games on tape delay on Channel 10, and even though the games had already been played, it didn't matter to me. Every pass, every fast break, and every roar of the crowd sparked something in my chest. I'd imagine myself out there, wearing that iconic blue and gray, running the floor in front of thousands of roaring fans at the Pyramid. In those quiet moments, with the crackle of the broadcast in the background, I'd dream of being a Tiger basketball player—one day hearing my name called and stepping onto that court. It was more than watching a game; it was a vision of what could be.

HARD LESSONS AND HAY FIELDS

Summers brought a different kind of magic: hay baling season. That's when Dad's friends, a robust and colorful group of buddies, would come over—James Dennie, Fummie Dennie, and Jim Hamlington—to help haul square bales under the scorching sun. I was too small to lift bales, so they put me in charge of driving the truck. It was an old stick shift, and I learned on the fly. I stalled, I jerked, and I got yelled at. But eventually, I figured it out.

Dad's buddies used colorful language occasionally, and I soaked up every word but knew better than to repeat them. Dad warned, "I better not ever hear you say them, and Mom better never hear it either." And he wasn't lying. One day, while walking with Mom near the creek, something moved in the brush. I shouted, "Mom, what the hell is that?" Her face froze. She yanked me back home and washed my mouth out with yellow Dial soap. I never cursed in front of her again.

George and I had a pact: what happened in the hayfields, stayed in the hayfields. One summer, George decided he wanted to try dip, just like the men. Dad warned him he'd regret it but let him try. James handed him a pinch, and George went full tough guy—spitting, nodding, saying he was fine until he wasn't. True to his nature, George was determined not to show any signs of weakness. I found him pale and sick behind a hay bale. But when Dad asked if he threw up, George lied through his teeth and said no, then went right back to stacking hay. That was George—stubborn, proud, and tough as nails. He never wanted to show weakness. I admired that about him, even if it sometimes got him into trouble.

Those summers taught me more than any classroom ever could. I learned how to work, respect effort, and be part of a team. I learned that the smallest kid on the farm could still earn a place at the table. That feeling of belonging and earning respect through sweat and grit stayed with me long after the last bale of hay was stacked.

Every memory, from the taste of Dial soap to the roar of Memphis fans on a delayed broadcast, formed the foundation of who I became. A small-town kid with big dreams, a deep faith, and a relentless work ethic—ready to chase the improbable.

CHAPTER 3

The Root Mentality

"Storms don't break people with deep roots."
Root

Sports were a part of our lives from the very beginning. Mom and Dad had signed us up for anything and everything we showed interest in—soccer, basketball, baseball, track—you name it, we probably tried it at some point. However, there was one non-negotiable rule: once you started something, you had to finish it. No quitting. No exceptions.

Looking back, that lesson might have been one of the greatest gifts they gave us. It didn't matter if the season wasn't going the way you wanted or if playing time was limited—if you committed, you saw it through. Period. That was how a Root operated. And long before I knew it, that simple rule would shape the way I approached not just sports, but life.

Discipline was the backbone of our family. Mom and Dad believed firmly in structure, in teaching right from wrong, in holding us accountable for our choices. They weren't our friends—they were our parents. And their job wasn't to make life easy for us; it was to prepare us for the world. "Because I said so" was a good enough reason for us when we asked our parents why.

Mom had a favorite saying anytime we left the house: "Remember, you're representing God, your family, and yourself." That was her daily reminder that we carried something bigger than ourselves everywhere we went. Our actions mattered because we reflected the people who raised us, the faith we claimed, and the family name on our backs.

And if we forgot that…well, there was always the wooden spoon.

That spoon was legendary in our house. It doubled as a cooking utensil and an enforcement tool. My siblings and I still laugh about being "wooden spoon survivors." I'll never forget the time Mom grabbed it to stir tea while guests were over, and I blurted out, "Mom, you can't use that! That's what you spank us with!" The room fell silent until one of the guests chuckled, "Nona, we use the same thing." Turns out, we weren't the only ones.

Those little moments were the roots being planted. Lessons that stuck. The older I get, the more I'm convinced the world could use a few more wooden spoons.

There's a fine line between discipline and discouragement. Mom and Dad never crossed it. They weren't overbearing—they were consistent. They didn't take sports away when we messed up. They took video games, phone time, or hanging out with friends, but never sports. Sports were sacred in our house. They taught accountability, commitment, and teamwork. Why would you punish a kid by removing the very thing that instills those lessons?

They did make that mistake once. My brother, George, got a bad grade in junior high, and basketball was taken away for a while. Years later, they admitted they regretted that decision. It didn't just punish George—it punished his team. It took away the very thing that helped him develop the discipline they were trying to teach.

That stuck with me.

But discipline wasn't the only thing our parents emphasized. They taught us to forgive. Always.

"Forgive, forget, move on," Mom would say. And Dad would remind us, "If you hold a grudge, they win twice—once when they hurt you and again when they live rent-free in your head."

Forgiveness didn't mean you had to stay close to someone who hurt you. It didn't mean you had to be a doormat. But it did mean you had to release bitterness—for your own peace, not theirs. Embracing

THE ROOT MENTALITY

forgiveness has enabled me to focus on personal growth and move forward with confidence and clarity.

And actions? They always spoke louder than words. It's important to always remember that a person's actions, or non-actions, speak louder than their words. Words can be empty, but actions reveal the true character and intentions of a person. Forgiveness was about freeing yourself, but wisdom was about setting boundaries.

Of all the things they taught us, though, the most important might have been this: Dream big.

Big dreams weren't just encouraged, they were expected. But dreaming without goals? That was just wishing.

One of my favorite quotes to this day comes from Denzel Washington: "Dreams without goals are just dreams. And ultimately, they fuel disappointment. On the road to achieving your dreams, you must apply discipline, but more importantly, consistency. Because without commitment, you'll never start, but without consistency, you'll never finish."

Mom and Dad were big believers in that idea long before I ever heard Denzel say it.

Dream. Set a goal. Chase it with everything you've got. Be consistent. Outwork everybody.

That was the Root way.

Over time, all these lessons blended together into what I now refer to as **The Root Mentality**.

It's simple, really.

It's about being grounded in who you are and where you come from. Like the roots of a mighty oak tree, the deeper they go, the stronger you stand when the storms of life come.

Roots keep you steady when the winds pick up. They feed you when life feels dry. They remind you of who you are when the world tries to tell you otherwise.

That's what Mom and Dad gave us. They gave us roots.

Strong ones.

Roots built on faith.

ROOT

Roots built on discipline.
Roots built on forgiveness.
Roots built on dreaming big, but also working big.
Roots that taught us:

- Start what you finish.
- Own your mistakes.
- Keep your word.
- Let your actions speak louder than anything you say.
- Never quit because it's hard.
- And always remember where you came from.

Those roots are why I could leave a small farm in McNairy County, Tennessee, and chase a dream in the city of Memphis.
Those roots are why I could handle disappointment and failure without falling apart.
Those roots are why I'm proud of the person I've become.
Because no matter where life takes me…
I'll always be grounded.
I'll always be rooted.
And I wouldn't have it any other way.

CHAPTER 4

Voices of My Foundation

"A good coach can change a game. A great coach can change a life."
JOHN WOODEN

Long before I ever stepped into the Pyramid in a Memphis jersey, I was shaped by men who saw more in me than I saw in myself. Coaches like Van Vansandt, and Steve Gagyi, and leaders like Fr. Carl Hood gave me a foundation deeper than basketball, rooted in faith, character, and belief. They taught me how to compete, but more importantly, how to lead with humility, how to prepare with purpose, and how to show up with heart, even when the odds were stacked against me.

As my Memphis career progressed, I found myself drawing on those early lessons more than ever. The roar of the crowd, the weight of each possession, and the physical grind, along with the emotional highs and lows—none of it would have meant as much, or been survivable, without the resilience those mentors had instilled in me. They weren't just preparing me to play the game. They were preparing me for life.

Nobody left a mark on me early in life quite like Coach Van. He was the local Church of Christ preacher, and he had this rare ability to lead with both strength and joy. He was a man who carried his love for God into every aspect of his life, including his passion for kids and sports, especially basketball. That voice—deep, booming, but full of warmth—you could hear from anywhere in the gym.

He coached me in Jr. Pro basketball from fourth through sixth grade.

And even as a fourth grader going up against sixth graders, he never let me back down from a challenge. He expected toughness. Effort. Hustle. And he believed in me. His confidence in my abilities made me believe in myself, and he always encouraged me to push past my limits.

I'll never forget my very first Jr. Pro game. Right before tip-off, Coach Van looked me dead in the eyes and told me I was jumping center. I thought for sure he was joking. I wasn't even the tallest on our team. But he smiled and said, "It's not about height, Root. It's about who gets off the floor quicker."

That confidence was all I needed. I jumped, won the tip, and from that day forward, the opening tip was my job.

Coach Van taught me early on that sometimes in life, someone else believing in you before you believe in yourself can change everything. That experience taught me an important lesson—sometimes, it's not about the obvious qualities people see, but about the belief someone else has in you that makes all the difference.

Fr. Carl Hood played a quiet yet powerful role in shaping my Catholic faith as I grew up. He had this rare ability to make the sacred feel both reverent and personal. Whether he was celebrating Mass or attending youth conventions with us, he made you feel like you mattered to him, and more importantly, to God.

What I loved most about Fr. Carl was that he wasn't just holy, he was funny. He could drop a one-liner in the middle of a homily that made the whole congregation laugh, then follow it with a truth that hit you right in the heart. He had a way of making faith approachable, reminding us that joy was just as much a part of the Gospel as sacrifice.

He helped me understand that the Catholic faith wasn't about checking boxes—it was about relationship. About showing up. About trusting God even when you didn't have all the answers. Fr. Carl didn't just preach that; he lived it. And through his example, I began to believe that maybe I could too.

By the time I reached sixth grade, my Dixie Youth days were coming to an end. That spring was going to be our last baseball season before junior high sports took over.

Coach Gagyi, whose son Derek was an absolute stud pitcher, drafted me with his second pick. He wanted me to catch Derek. I had barely caught up the year before, but he saw something in me.

That season turned into one of my all-time favorite memories in sports because of one crazy game plan that to this day still makes me laugh.

We were playing the other team from our small town. Big rivalry game. We were up 3-0 heading into the last inning, but there was one huge problem.

One of our players hadn't gotten his required at-bat.

If we won without him batting, we'd have to forfeit.

Coach Gagyi calmly told Derek and me what we had to do: Get the first two outs fast. Then...start letting them score.

Nobody else knew. Our parents and other fans were shouting in confusion.

We got two quick outs, then Derek started walking batters on purpose. A couple of hits later, the game was tied. Once it was, Derek struck out the final batter, and we went to extra innings. We got our missing guy his at-bat and then shut them down to win the game.

That moment taught me that sometimes in life, strategy, patience, and teamwork matter more than raw talent.

Looking back, those three taught me way more than just sports and faith. I know it wasn't a coincidence. God brought the right mentors into my life at just the right time. God's timing is always perfect, even when it doesn't align with ours.

- Coach Van taught me the importance of belief and toughness.
- Fr. Hood gave me the confidence to embrace my Catholic faith.
- Coach Gagyi taught me teamwork and strategy.

They all shaped me in ways I didn't even realize at the time.

They cared about us as people more than they cared about wins.

And all these years later, their lessons stuck with me far longer than any score or trophy.

That's the thing about great mentors: you may forget the final record, but you never forget the way they made you feel. You never forget the memories.

These men—Fr. Carl Hood, Van Vansandt, and Steve Gagyi—didn't just coach me in youth sports or help grow my faith.

They mentored me for life.

CHAPTER 5

Lessons from the Legends

"Every small town has legends. I was lucky enough to grow up among mine."
Root

Growing up near a small town, sports were just part of our DNA. My earliest coaches, like Eddie McDaniel, Steve Gagyi, and Van Vansandt, were the first to shape me beyond my parents.

But as much as those coaches shaped me, my greatest classroom came just down the road at the corner of Main Street (Hwy 64) and Hwy 117—the local YMCA. Situated at the corner of the only red light in town, the YMCA was more than just a building—it was a hub for the community's youth.

If the farm was my home, the Y was my second home.

After school, that's where you'd find me. And it didn't matter how young or small you were—if you were willing to get out there and play hard, the older guys would let you run. And man, the older guys were legends in my eyes. Guys like Matt Hoover, Russ Kennamore, Jonathan "Bubba" Hoover, Rob Bullington, Lamont Robinson, J.T. Livezey, and Doug Rogers. Some ended up being high school stars and college players. They were all the coolest guys in town, and for me, they set the standard I wanted to reach.

These guys didn't just influence how I played—they influenced who I became. Through countless hours at the YMCA, I began to understand the kind of player—and, more importantly, the kind of person I wanted to become. They challenged me to be better, and their influence helped shape me into a more competitive and disciplined individual.

Matt and Russ were the first two I really watched closely. Russ was the smooth one—quick, athletic, just a natural. He played with a confidence that looked effortless. He was fearless, and I soaked that up like a sponge. Matt, on the other hand, was built like an athlete from the jump—tall, long, 6'6", but with guard skills. Watching him handle the ball and shoot with ease at that size was unbelievable. They were like Jordan and Pippen in our little gym.

And then there was Bubba—the sharpshooter.

If Russ and Matt showed me how to play, Bubba showed me how to work and how to carry myself. Loyal. Tough. Joyful. Bubba was everybody's favorite person because he made every room better just by walking in. He was quick with a joke, competitive to the core, and would fight for his people.

My mom used to tell this story about Bubba from when she taught him in fifth grade. She had assigned the class to write a funny poem. Bubba delivered this gem:

"Going down the highway, hitting 64,
Dexter let a big one and blew me out the door."

Mom was horrified but also cried with laughter. In bright red ink, she wrote: "Jonathan, this is inappropriate!"

To this day, we still joke about that line every time Bubba does something classic Bubba.

But Bubba was more than funny; he had this rare combination of heart and toughness. He was the first guy to check on you if you were down. The first to pat you on the back when you got it right. And if he told you he had your back, you could take it to the bank.

Rob Bullington was another guy I learned from—small in stature but tough as nails. He never backed down from a challenge. Football was his sport, but he was always in the Y, hooping with us, scrapping

LESSONS FROM THE LEGENDS

for every rebound, diving on every loose ball. Rob taught me it's not about size—it's about heart. His attitude had a huge influence on me. Watching Rob fight through obstacles and push himself to be better, even when the odds weren't in his favor, taught me the importance of toughness and perseverance.

Lamont Robinson, man... he was just one of a kind. The best storyteller I've ever known. He had this way of walking into any room and owning it within five minutes. He had a hustler's mentality—in a good way. Resourceful, loyal, and able to talk to anyone about anything. Lamont taught me about presence, confidence, and how to adapt to people in the room, regardless of the environment I found myself in.

Doug Rogers might not have been the best athlete, but he was absolutely part of our crew. Doug didn't miss a game, didn't miss a hangout, didn't miss a chance to support his people. His younger brother, Luke, was a great athlete, but Doug was the heartbeat of the group off the court. Loyal to the core. That mattered to me.

As the crow flies, Doug lived only about two miles from our farm, and it always felt like he was just a part of our everyday life. Whether he was hanging out after practices, cheering us on from the stands, or just being there to support his friends, Doug's loyalty and constant presence made him a valued part of the group.

And then there was J.T.

J.T. didn't move to our school until his freshman year, but even then, his reputation was already solid. Hard worker. Tough. But also, a loyal friend. We didn't get close until later in life, but I always respected his work ethic. He taught me you could grind and still have fun doing it.

Each of these guys shaped me in a different way.

Rob showed me toughness. Lamont showed me swagger. Doug showed me loyalty. J.T. showed me work ethic. Russ showed me confidence. Matt showed me skill. Bubba showed me heart.

The YMCA was more than a gym—it was my proving ground. My classroom. My playground. And those guys? They were my teachers.

ROOT

They didn't even know it most of the time. They were just being themselves. But man, I was watching. I was learning.

And to this day, if you ask me who shaped me as a player and a person, it wasn't just my parents or my coaches. It was those long afternoons at the Y, getting beat up by the older guys, getting encouraged by them, learning how to hold my own, how to compete, and how to belong.

Those were the days that built me.

Those were the guys who raised me.

And the best part? All these years later… they're still my friends.

Still my people.

Still my roots.

CHAPTER 6

The Start of a Powerhouse

*"When you realize nothing is guaranteed,
every opportunity becomes sacred."*
Root

During the winter, Friday nights in the gym weren't just about basketball. They were about belonging. They were about dreaming. They were about a community that lived and died for our boys' basketball team.

As a sixth grader sitting in those packed wooden bleachers, squeezed between upperclassmen in the student section, I wasn't just watching the game—I was studying it. Soaking it in. Imagining what it would feel like one day to run out of that locker room, wearing that red and white jersey, hearing my name over the loudspeaker.

That dream only intensified as I got older.

The 1993 season, with Russ leading the charge and guiding our hometown team to its first-ever state tournament appearance, was just the beginning. The very next year, a sharpshooter named Seth Massey picked up the torch and led us right back. And then came Matt and Bubba—their turn to lead. Not only did they take us back to the state tournament, but they also carried us all the way to the state championship game, finishing as state runners-up. And all of us younger guys? We were watching their every move, just waiting for our chance to write our own chapter in the story they had started.

Basketball in our town wasn't just a sport—it was part of the culture.

ROOT

It was woven into the fabric of Friday nights in small-town Tennessee. There was just something different about our little gym. Perhaps it was the intimacy—with barely 1,000 seats—or maybe it was the pride of a close-knit community rallying around its youth.

Whatever it was, it created an environment unlike anything I've ever experienced since.

Visiting teams hated playing against us. Our student section was ruthless, creative, and absolutely relentless. It didn't matter if it was a district opponent or a state-ranked powerhouse—when you walked into that gym, you were in for a war. The combination of our talented team and our fiercely loyal fans created an atmosphere that made it one of the toughest places to play in the state.

And the beauty of it was, we traveled like that, too. Home or away, it didn't matter. Our fans showed up. Our student section showed up. Those games left a lasting impression on me, not just because of the incredible basketball being played, but because of the sense of community and pride that our small town had for its team. It made me realize how much sports can bring people together and how much it meant to represent something bigger than yourself.

That was the world I was growing up in—chasing dreams inside that little gym, idolizing the older guys I watched dominate on Friday nights, and spending every spare minute at the YMCA trying to sharpen my own game.

And then, out of nowhere, life hit pause.

It was just an ordinary afternoon. A typical school day that ended like so many others had—George, Natalie, and I at the Y after school while Mom ran her usual taxi service, picking us up and shuttling us around.

That day, George had practice back at the junior/senior high school, so after dropping him off, Mom turned the van toward home with Natalie and me in tow. That drive home was second nature to us—same road, same turns, same little markers we passed every single day.

Until it wasn't.

Coming around that curve—the one Mom always slowed down for—life changed in a split second.

THE START OF A POWERHOUSE

One minute, I was turning my head to check for cars, as I always did…and the next, I heard her scream.

A flash of metal. Headlights. And then impact.

I don't remember the actual collision. One second, I was bracing; the next, I was hanging over the seatbelt, my heart pounding, my ears ringing. The first thing I heard was Mom's voice—calm, somehow.

"Nathaniel, are you okay?"

I told her I was. Truth is, I was in shock. But her next words snapped me into action.

"Get out of the van and get your sister out. I'm trapped."

Instinct kicked in. I scrambled out, yanked the side door open, and pulled Natalie to safety. I'll never forget the panic in my voice as I screamed for help, watching neighbors run from their homes, seeing Mom pinned inside, hearing someone yell about leaking gas.

But then—like only a mother could—she managed to free herself. Bruised, battered, but moving.

I rushed to her side, helping her away from the wreckage. Relief washed over me like a wave. We were alive.

Looking back now, I realize how lucky we were. A few broken ribs. Some stitches. Bruises and burns from seatbelts doing their job. But it could have been so much worse.

God's hand was on us that day—no doubt about it. Our guardian angels were there with us, present and protecting us from serious harm.

That accident became a permanent marker in my life. A moment that reminded me how fragile it all really is. That the dreams I was chasing weren't promised. That every day, every game, every practice, and every chance to get better mattered.

And maybe that's why the dream burned even brighter after that.

Surviving something like that changes you, even at a young age. It sharpens your focus. It reminds you that life can turn in an instant. And for me, it gave everything I was chasing—every goal, every dream—just a little more urgency.

Because I knew—in a way most sixth graders didn't—how quickly it could all be taken away.

Thankfully, that wreck didn't derail what was happening back at the high school. The run we were about to go on was just getting started.

That first trip to the state tournament had lit the fire. The next few years would fan it into an all-out blaze.

Every kid in our town wanted to wear that jersey. Every kid wanted to run out of that locker room to a packed house, representing something bigger than themselves.

And me?

I wasn't just dreaming about it anymore.

I was dead set on making it happen.

CHAPTER 7

Foundations of Determination

*"True character is revealed not when you're at the top,
but when you're benched and still choose to lead."*
Root

The following summer brought even more growth, both on and off the court. My confidence had started to build, not just from basketball success or working alongside my dad, but from the quiet victories, the internal ones that come when you begin to understand who you are and where you're going.

I started working with my dad whenever I could, stacking bricks, hauling mortar, and mixing concrete. I wasn't afraid of hard work, so when he offered, I jumped at the chance. It was honest, backbreaking work, but I knew it was shaping me. I didn't always love it in the moment, but I always loved the feeling of finishing a job. Standing back with my dad and seeing a wall or set of steps we built together—that pride never got old. I started to understand why he held such high standards. He wasn't just teaching me masonry; he was teaching me how to show up in life.

I can still feel the sting of those early summer mornings—the kind of heat that clings to your skin before the sun even fully rises. By 6:00 a.m., we were already on the job site, and by 7:00 a.m., my shirt was soaked through, my hands caked in mortar, dust, and sweat from hauling bricks, pushing heavy wheelbarrows full of wet mortar, and stacking block after block. But somewhere in the grind, I could feel something happening—not just in my arms or shoulders, but inside of me. Every load I carried was doing more than building a house. It was building me and strengthening not just my body, but my resolve.

Dad didn't cut me any slack just because I was his son. In fact, most days it felt like he was even harder on me because of it. He held me to the same standard as every other guy on that job site—maybe even higher. If I wasn't working hard enough, he let me know. If I wasn't paying attention, I heard about it. And now, looking back, I know exactly why he did it. He wasn't just trying to teach me how to lay brick or mix mortar; he was teaching me how to work and how to show up and get the job done. He wasn't raising a laborer; he was raising a man.

As summer gave way to fall, my parents surprised me with a decision I never expected—they finally agreed to let me play football. Up to that point, they'd been firm in saying no, being worried about injuries. But after enough pleading from my older brother, they caved, and I suited up for my first—and what would be my only—season.

Our junior high coach doubled as the high school baseball coach and was known for his no-nonsense intensity. He didn't need to yell much because his presence alone demanded your full effort. If you didn't bring it, he let you hear about it, plain and simple.

Our team wasn't great, and it didn't take long for me to realize football wasn't my sport. But quitting was never an option in our house. So I stuck it out, gave it my all, and finished the season. It wasn't about stats or wins, it was about honoring the commitment I made when I put on the helmet.

When November rolled around, it meant one thing: basketball season. After grinding through a long football season, I was more than ready to get back to the sport I loved most.

We had a new coach that year, and with over 20 guys trying out between seventh and eighth graders, I knew nothing was guaranteed. Jr. Pro felt like a distant memory now. This was junior high, and if I wanted to play and start, I was going to have to earn it.

But those long, hot days working with Dad that summer had

prepared me for moments just like this. I didn't back down. I showed up every day, battled through every drill, and worked like crazy to prove I belonged.

And before long, all that effort paid off. When the season tipped off, I wasn't just playing, I was starting. The only seventh grader in the starting five. It didn't come easily, but that made it even sweeter. Every drop of sweat, every brick hauled that summer, had led me here.

The Christmas break that year brought a much-needed pause from practices and games. And on December 30th, we had big plans. My mom, a die-hard Memphis fan, had gotten tickets for us to see the University of Tennessee women's basketball team take on the Memphis Lady Tigers at the Pyramid Arena.

She called her brother, my Uncle Ned—a Tennessee fan through and through—and of course, he jumped at the chance to see the legendary Pat Summitt coach in person.

We'd been to Memphis plenty of times growing up, visiting family, but this was different. This was the Pyramid—32 stories tall, rising up from the banks of the Mississippi like a monument. As we pulled into the parking lot that afternoon, I was mesmerized. The sheer size of it took my breath away.

Before the van had even come to a full stop, I threw open the door and stepped out, staring straight up at that massive building. And without hesitation—with the kind of certainty only a young kid with a dream can have—I turned to my family and said, "I am home. I will play in this arena one day."

I didn't just hope for it. I believed it. That moment planted a dream in my heart that would never leave.

After Christmas break, it was back to the grind. I felt like I was finally hitting my stride. I was playing solid, scoring in double figures a few times, and settling into my role. However, as a team, we weren't living up to expectations. Something had to change.

That's when the coach made a move that floored me; he pulled me and another starter from the lineup and moved me to the sixth-man role.

I was crushed. It stung. But after talking with my brother and Bubba, their advice stuck with me: "Use this. When you get in, play so hard he can't take you out."

So that's exactly what I did. I embraced it. Every time I checked in, I played with an edge—diving for loose balls, guarding like my life depended on it, and bringing energy every possession.

We finished dead last in the county in the regular season—the lowest of lows. No team had ever gone from last place to winning the county tournament. But somehow, we flipped a switch. When the tournament started, we played our best basketball of the year, rattling off three straight wins to capture the county championship.

Looking back, I realized my coach didn't bench me because I wasn't playing well; he benched me because he needed a spark, and he believed I could be that guy. It taught me an invaluable lesson: sometimes life calls you to play a different role. And when that moment comes, it's not about pride, it's about doing whatever it takes to help your team win.

As our season wrapped up in late January, all eyes in town shifted to the high school team, and for me, it meant even more now that my brother, George, was a freshman playing for them. Watching the varsity guys had always been a big deal, but now I wasn't just watching my heroes, I was watching my brother.

That year, our high school team was on a roll, playing some of the best basketball we had seen in years. And nothing brought more excitement than a rivalry game against McNairy Central. The schools didn't like each other—plain and simple—and those games were always electric.

I'll never forget sitting in the packed student section that night, surrounded by all the older kids. One of their traditions was crowd-surfing me through the stands because I was small enough to lift over their heads; it made me feel like I was part of the team even though I wasn't on the court.

As the teams walked to center court for the jump ball, McNairy's student section started chanting: "Too many white boys! Clap, clap!

FOUNDATIONS OF DETERMINATION

Too many white boys!" They were mocking our mostly white lineup, except for one player, Alonzo Sutton.

They didn't chant for long.

Alonzo easily won the tip, and within a few passes, the ball found Preston Brooks, one of our senior forwards. Preston ripped through on the baseline, took two hard dribbles, and rose up with authority, hammering down a monster two-handed dunk that shook the gym.

The place absolutely exploded.

That dunk silenced McNairy's student section and lit a fire under our guys. We played with an edge the rest of the night, eventually pulling away for one of the sweetest wins I can remember.

It was the kind of night that reminded me why I loved basketball—the energy, the pride, the noise, and the moments you never forget.

Every time I watched those older guys take the court, I'd imagine myself out there with them. The roar of the crowd, the sweat-soaked jerseys, and the intensity of every possession called to me.

But it wasn't just the game I admired. It was the way they carried themselves. There was something different about the way those teams walked, the way they talked, and the way they competed. It wasn't arrogance. It was purpose. They knew they were part of something bigger. And every young kid in that gym—myself included—wanted to feel what they were feeling.

CHAPTER 8

Strength Through Adversity

"Control what you can control. Let the rest go."
ROOT

As my seventh grade year ended, all eyes in our little town were once again on the high school basketball team. Another trip to the state tournament had the whole community buzzing. Still, for me, it also meant shifting my focus back to baseball and getting ready for another summer working alongside my dad.

That summer moved fast—a blur of ball games, practices, and long, hot days on the job site. There was never a dull moment. Between sports and stacking bricks, I stayed busy, learning lessons in both places that would stick with me for life.

When eighth grade rolled around, I was done with football for good. I knew my heart was in basketball, and I was all in. Baseball was still fun, but it had taken a back seat. My real passion lived inside that gym.

George was now a sophomore on the high school team, and even though their official practices hadn't started yet, they'd stay after school playing pickup games, and I couldn't get down there fast enough. Every day when that final bell rang, I'd sprint to the gym hoping somebody needed an extra body. And most days, I lucked out.

Getting to play against the older guys was like stepping into a different world. They were bigger, stronger, and smarter, and I loved every second of it. George still owned me in one-on-one games. It drove me crazy. He wasn't necessarily a better scorer, but defensively, he had me figured out. He knew my moves before I made them, and he took pride in shutting me down.

At the time, I thought he was just being a typical big brother, trying to embarrass me. But looking back now, I know exactly what he was doing. He, Bubba, Matt, and the rest of those guys were sharpening me. Toughening me up. Preparing me for what was next.

By early November, basketball season was officially here. Our junior high team practiced early in the mornings, which meant that after school, I was free to hang around the high school practices. And I soaked up every bit of it.

This high school team was special. After back-to-back state tournament appearances, they weren't just playing for a good season; they were chasing a state title.

Matt, now a senior, was the best player our school had ever seen. Standing 6'6" or 6'7", he could do it all. Score, rebound, defend—the game came easily to him. And then there was Bubba, a junior and the team's sharpshooter. His ability to catch fire from beyond the arc could change a game in an instant. Together, Matt and Bubba were the heartbeat of that team.

Watching those practices taught me something deeper than X's and O's. It taught me what greatness looked like up close—the work, the focus, and the relentless drive.

That November, they had a scrimmage over in Bolivar, Tennessee. Afterwards, the team planned to head to Trenton Peabody to watch Rob Bullington and Chad Wyatt play in the football playoffs. Chad was our starting point guard. I begged to tag along. Thankfully, Coach said yes, and with George already on the team, my parents were fine with it.

That trip meant everything to me. Riding in that little chocolate-brown bus with the high school guys, I felt like I belonged—like I was getting my first taste of what it meant to truly be part of something bigger.

That night, watching Rob play, I saw toughness on full display. He was giving up inches and pounds to everybody on that field, but none of that mattered. He took one of the hardest hits I've ever seen and bounced right back up like it was nothing. That stuck with me. That was the kind of toughness I wanted in my own game.

As our junior high season got underway, things didn't exactly go as I hoped. We were average at best. We finished in the middle of the pack and lost early in the county tournament. But more than that, I struggled with my coach. His style and mine didn't mesh, and it made it hard to enjoy the game I loved so much.

It was one of the first real challenges I faced as a young athlete. I remember venting to my parents about it, unsure of how to handle the frustration. Their advice was simple but powerful:

> Control what you can control. Be a great teammate. Focus on getting better. Learn what you can, even from a coach you don't love. And most of all, stay positive. Better days are coming.

That mindset shift made all the difference. It taught me how to handle adversity without losing my love for the game.

Meanwhile, the high school team was putting together the best season in school history. They made it all the way to the state championship game, finishing as runners-up but leaving a legacy that inspired every kid coming up behind them. Matt, the heart and soul of that run, would go on to sign with Union University—just 45 minutes up the road—giving us all a reason to keep rooting for him.

When spring rolled around, baseball brought new life. Coach Ricky Coffman was exactly the type of coach I needed at that point. Calm, steady, approachable, but demanding. He got the best out of you without having to yell. And after a rough basketball season, his style helped me regain my confidence and love for competing.

That spring and summer, Coach Coffman helped me rebuild my confidence. I played hard, worked even harder, and kept building. I even figured out I needed contacts after losing too many balls in the light of the popcorn machine, which was located directly behind home plate.

ROOT

Looking back, my seventh and eighth grade years were filled with lessons that extended far beyond the scoreboard. Lessons about hard work, resilience, handling adversity, and surrounding yourself with people who make you better.

Every practice, every pickup game, every bus ride, and every long, hot day laying brick with my dad was all part of the foundation being built underneath me.

A foundation I would stand on for the rest of my life.

CHAPTER 9

The Road to 32

"It's not about being the next somebody. It's about being the first you."
ROOT

The summer before my freshman year looked a lot like the one before it—early mornings on the job site with Dad, mixing mortar, stacking blocks, and hauling whatever needed moving. The work was tough, but by now I had grown used to the rhythm: labor during the day, then straight to the gym to lift and work on my game. I could feel my body and mindset getting stronger.

That summer also marked a milestone for George—he turned sixteen and got his first car: a 1976 Chrysler New Yorker. I couldn't help but laugh when they pulled into the driveway. "It's a land yacht," I teased, refusing to be seen in it. My embarrassment was short-lived. Mom and Dad reminded me how fortunate I was to even have a ride, and if I wanted something better, I'd better start saving. So, I did. I opened a savings account and started stacking every dollar I earned. It was my first real lesson in independence and financial responsibility.

When school started, I was beyond excited to finally practice with the varsity basketball team during school hours. At our school, it was rare for freshmen to dress out for varsity games, but I knew there were a few open spots. That was all I needed to double down and push harder.

We opened with preseason conditioning—15 laps around the school's front yard to equal three miles. I knew George, a natural runner, would lead the pack, and if I could keep up, I'd be in good shape. The August heat was brutal, and about two miles in, Coach yelled, "Root, you really going to let your brother beat you?" That lit a fire. I surged past a few older guys and caught up to Bubba, who slapped me on the butt and told me to go get George. I never caught him, but I finished second and showed something that day—grit. The coaches saw it, and that mattered more than winning the run.

As the season neared, I had one of the most pivotal conversations of my young life. One Sunday night at the high school gym, a group of the older guys, who were back in town from college—Matt, Russ, Bubba, Rob, and Lamont—pulled me aside after a pickup game. When I casually mentioned a classmate's party, they got serious. They laid it out plain: no drinking, no smoking, and no girls if it meant losing focus. They weren't scolding—they were investing in me. I promised them that night I'd stay the course, and I meant it.

When the season began, I was one of the few freshmen to earn a varsity uniform. That feeling was everything. But three games in, I was left off the roster for a game against our rivals, Hardin County. The coach wanted to let a few freshmen from the Hardin County district suit up instead to inspire their community to send their kids to our school for sports. I understood the logic, but it stung. I was disappointed, frustrated, and honestly, a little hurt. It felt like all my effort had been overlooked in favor of a decision that wasn't based on merit. Still, I didn't let it derail me. I used it as fuel, and after that, I never missed another varsity game.

That season brought new challenges as well. We had moved from single A to double AA, meaning stiffer competition. Early injuries hit our team hard, but we still had some serious talent. Bubba, our sharp-shooting leader, and Anthony Brooks, a 6'9" force who was coming into his own, and Luke Rogers, Doug's younger brother who was easily our best athlete—his natural abilities on the court were unmatched—all kept us competitive. Both Anthony and Bubba signed early scholarships to play at Union University, following the path Matt had carved before them. Even though our season ended with a loss in the first round of regionals, I had grown in ways that went far beyond the win column.

I also made a personal change—cutting off my old bowl cut and going with a buzz like Bubba's. It was a small decision, but it felt like a shift in identity, like I was starting to step into my own.

Even though we ended that season with a loss in the first round of the regional championships, I still had plenty of fond memories to hold on to. It had been a year of growth and learning, and despite the ups and downs, I came away from it a better player.

I'll never forget one game when the coach meant to sub in Bubba but accidentally grabbed my head—thanks to our matching haircuts. I sprinted in, made a hustle play, and then got yanked for Bubba just a few seconds later. We laughed about it, but in those little moments, I learned patience and humility.

There were flashes of excitement too, like stealing the ball against Hardin County in the fourth quarter of a tight game. Bubba had four fouls on him, and Coach didn't want to risk him fouling out. During a timeout, Coach looked over at me, sizing up the situation. "If I put you in, can you get a steal?" he asked. I don't even remember if I answered him out loud, but in my mind, I was ready. Without hesitation, I turned and sprinted to the scorer's table to check into the game.

When the timeout ended, we broke the huddle, each of us finding the player we were assigned to guard. As the official handed the ball to one of Hardin County's players to inbound, I was glued to my man, determined not to let him get the ball. But then, I saw the pass go in—straight to their big guy. He fumbled the catch, and that was all I needed. I sprinted over, swiped the ball, and headed down the court.

In that moment, being a freshman, I didn't know what to do next, so I called a timeout. The film later showed I had a teammate wide open down the court. Another lesson: always keep your eyes up.

My teammates jumped up, patting me on the back and congratulating me for the steal. I felt a surge of excitement, but I quickly turned to Coach and said, "I got you a steal like you asked, now get Bubba back in the game." I knew the team needed him out there to finish the job.

Unfortunately, we didn't pull out the win that night. Not continuing the play taught me a valuable lesson. It taught me to trust my instincts and always be aware of what's happening around me on the court.

The highlight of my freshman year came at the spring sports banquet. I didn't expect any awards. I hadn't played much, and I was just glad to have suited up. But then Tracey Carter, one of our senior captains, stood at the mic to announce who would wear the leadership #32 jersey next season. Everyone assumed it would go to a rising senior. Instead, he said, "Next year, Nathaniel Root will be wearing the leadership #32 jersey."

I was stunned. That number was a badge of honor—worn only by the most trusted and respected captains of their teams. Players like Tracey Carter, Chad Wyatt, and Kevin McLain wore this jersey. I had looked up to the guys who wore it before me, and now, just a freshman, it was being passed down to me.

As that school year came to a close, I carried two things: pride in what I had accomplished and a deeper awareness of the responsibility ahead. Wearing #32 wasn't just a number—it was a statement. I wasn't the kid trying to prove he belonged anymore. I was now someone the others would expect to lead our proud program into the future.

And I was ready.

CHAPTER 10

Bonds Built, Brick by Brick

"You don't have to have it all figured out to lead. Sometimes, leadership means walking through the uncertainty with courage."
Root

I try not to dwell too much on my sophomore year—it was one of those seasons you'd rather forget. I entered the year with high hopes. We had some promising young talent, and I believed we could build something special. But not everyone shared that vision. A few of the older players—juniors and seniors—didn't appreciate the younger players showing up, competing for minutes, and potentially threatening their spots. The tension in the locker room was thick, and it never really went away.

We were still in double-A competition, which kept the stakes high. Every game was a battle, and not just against the other team. The real challenge often came from within as I tried to find my voice as a leader in a fractured locker room. I was the starting point guard, a sophomore expected to lead, and that pressure weighed on me daily.

We opened the season against Middleton, a former district rival with a history of tough, athletic teams. Middleton had always been an athletic team known for producing great talent, including Memphis Tiger great Bobby Parks, who played for the Tigers from 1980 to 1984. Our gym was packed, the energy was electric, and all eyes were on us—this new generation of young players trying to carry the torch. I was called out first during introductions and would hold that starting spot for the entire year. That night, we pulled out a gritty win, and it felt like a turning point. I thought it was the start of something special.

But things quickly unraveled. Practices turned into shouting matches. Fights broke out. The camaraderie we needed never materialized. I began questioning whether I was cut out for this kind of leadership. I should have been proud to start varsity as a sophomore, but the environment left me frustrated and worn down. I couldn't understand why the older guys didn't seem to care as much as I did.

Eventually, my mom noticed something was off. When she asked what was wrong, I gave her a brief glimpse into what was going on. I didn't go into detail—I believed in protecting the sanctity of the locker room—but she could sense the weight I was carrying. Her words were simple but powerful: "Son, this too shall pass." It became my anchor during a season that often felt like a storm.

One of the few bright spots was my growing friendship with Daniel Gibbs, a junior sharpshooter. We found common ground in our frustration and used it to fuel a shared commitment: we'd spend the off-season rebuilding, holding ourselves and our teammates accountable. That promise kept me focused, giving me hope that we could change the culture going forward.

After basketball season, I didn't return to baseball. Instead, I joined our school's brand-new soccer program—our first ever. It was George's senior year, and he decided to play too, signing on as our goalie while I was named starting forward. We weren't great—our season was winless—but the experience was still fun. We were a group of athletes from various sports trying to build something new from scratch.

A few games in, George broke his arm. He still played in the field with a padded cast, but someone had to take over in goal. That someone was me. I didn't want the role—it reminded me of baseball, when I decided not to play anymore because of the slow pace. But this time, I decided to do it for my brother. I did what the team needed.

In hindsight, I'm glad I did. George ended up scoring the first goal in the history of our program. Seeing him celebrate that moment made every frustration worth it.

BONDS BUILT, BRICK BY BRICK

Looking back now, my sophomore year was filled with hard lessons. It challenged me in ways I wasn't prepared for—testing my leadership, forcing me to adapt, and reminding me that not every season goes according to plan. But through the friction, disappointment, and unexpected roles, I grew. I learned to persevere, to lead with humility, and to focus on the long game. It wasn't the year I had envisioned, but it was the year that started to shape the kind of leader I would become.

The summer between my sophomore and junior year felt like a reset button. I was back working long days with Dad, but this time, I wasn't doing it alone. Dad had taken on a big bricklaying job and needed an extra hand, so I asked Daniel—my teammate and closest friend from the season before—if he wanted to join us. He didn't hesitate.

We built our routine quickly. I'd wake up at 4:30 a.m., pack a lunch, and by 5:10, we'd be heading to the job site. Daniel was always waiting early, eager to work. The labor was brutal, especially under the summer sun, but we didn't mind. We worked side by side, hauling blocks and mixing mortar, pushing each other physically while dreaming big about the season ahead. Dad had to tell us more than once to stop talking and get back to work. But in truth, that summer built more than muscle—it solidified a bond.

Once work was done by mid-afternoon, we weren't finished. We'd shower, meet up at the gym, and grind—lifting, playing one-on-one, and shooting until the lights went out. We were determined: Daniel to have a great senior year, and I to step into my role more as the team leader.

When school resumed, we got unexpected news: our enrollment had dropped, moving us back to single-A competition. We were back where we belonged, and our team was stacked. Deep at every position, we could rotate 10 or 12 guys. For me, that meant playing the pass-first point guard role—facilitating, sacrificing shots for the good of the team.

But deep down, I worried. I dreamed of playing at Memphis, and scorers got noticed. If I wasn't putting up numbers, how would I catch a scout's eye? The pressure to perform, even in limited minutes, was real. I knew I had to excel in other areas, specifically with my assist-to-turnover ratio. If I could prove that I could distribute the ball with precision and make smart decisions under pressure, maybe that would be enough.

I was also in a battle for my starting spot. A senior transfer had become eligible and wanted the job I had earned the year before. I edged him out before game one, but just barely. One mistake and I could be riding the bench. It created a strange feeling—wanting your team to succeed but also watching your replacement, hoping for a slip-up so you could get back in. The whole season played out like that—one mistake and you were out of the game, sitting on the bench, watching your replacement.

We played an exciting, fast-paced brand of basketball—pressuring, running, scoring in transition—and we were winning. But midway through the season, I felt a soreness in my foot. I tried to ignore it, but it got worse with each game. Finally, the pain was too much to push through. A bone scan confirmed it: a stress fracture. I'd be out two to four weeks.

I was crushed. All that work, gone in an instant. My injury was something completely beyond my control, and that was the hardest part to accept. Watching from the sidelines was torture. I tried to lead from the bench, but it wasn't the same. After four weeks, I was cleared to return, but not to my starting spot. The coach told me I'd be coming off the bench. I had worked so hard to earn my starting spot, and now, because of an injury, I was being relegated to a lesser role. It felt like a slap in the face. I felt like I was being punished for getting injured. I didn't agree with it, but I accepted the role and made the most of it.

In my first game back, I was filled with adrenaline and pent-up energy. Our team jumped out to an early lead, and I sat on the bench, eagerly waiting for my chance to get back on the court. Finally, toward the end of the first quarter, I got my opportunity. The crowd erupted in cheers for my return. It was an amazing feeling, but I had to keep my focus.

BONDS BUILT, BRICK BY BRICK

I settled in quickly and got right to work, playing like I hadn't missed a beat. In fewer minutes, playing a lesser role, I had scored my career-high of 18 points. For a pass-first point guard coming off injury, it felt huge. I was proving I could still contribute, even in a reduced role.

We cruised through district play and won the district tournament with ease. Regionals were tougher, but we rose to the occasion and won three straight to claim the region title. During that stretch, I played some of my best basketball, and to my surprise, was named to the all-region team. It was validation. Everything I'd poured into the season—the early mornings, the grind with Daniel, the recovery—it had meant something.

That set up a home sub-state game with a trip to the state tournament on the line. By the time we arrived at the gym that evening, there was already a line of fans stretching outside the school, eager to get the best seats. The gym was packed—standing room only, buzzing with anticipation. I'd never heard our place that loud. The atmosphere felt like it was leading to something special.

And for most of the game, it was. We held the lead deep into the fourth. But a late-game collapse—layups we couldn't stop, a costly technical foul—flipped the momentum. We never switched to a zone defense, which might have helped. And just like that, our state dreams slipped away.

The locker room after the game was heavy. The pain of the loss hit hard. I hugged Daniel, both of us fighting back tears. We had poured everything into this season. Now it was over. That final embrace, the silent understanding between teammates who had worked, suffered, and believed, meant more than any scoreboard ever could. Although the season ended in disappointment, the journey was one of growth, sacrifice, and enduring bonds.

CHAPTER 11

Confronting the Unexpected

"Courage is not the absence of fear, but the triumph over it."
NELSON MANDELA

Leaving basketball behind and shifting to soccer wasn't easy. I kept replaying the final loss in my mind, knowing only three teams in the state got to end their season with a win. Everyone else was left with the sting of what-ifs. But that sting soon gave way to a new fire.

This time, our soccer team wasn't starting from scratch—we had experience. There was a different kind of energy around us. We set clear goals: score more, win more, and make a mark. And we did. We won our first games, and though I was still in the goalie position I hadn't asked for, I embraced the role. The season flew by, and with it came a quiet sense of accomplishment. We were building something.

Heading into my senior basketball season, our confidence was sky-high. We'd lost a few key players but still had depth and chemistry. To test us, our coach signed us up for an AAU tournament in Memphis, where the best of the best played. We walked in full of belief and walked out with three humbling losses. No matter how good we were in rural West Tennessee, we were no match for the top players in Memphis when they joined forces. It was the wake-up call we needed. Winning in our area was one thing; competing against combined Memphis talent was another. From that point on, we attacked the gym with new intensity.

That summer, Matt and Bubba—both now playing at Union—pulled me aside and said, "If you're serious about playing in college, come join us in pickup games at Union." I jumped at the chance, and my parents agreed. They trusted the Hoover family like they trusted their own, and they knew I needed to stretch myself against college competition. They also knew that Doc and M.L. Hoover, Matt and Bubba's parents, would be there most of the time, keeping an eye on us. And they trusted that if I ever stepped out of line, the Hoovers would treat me as if I were their own child.

These games were a whole different level of competition. They were a whole new world—faster, sharper, and filled with future mentors. Gaylon Moore and Steve Poindexter stood out not just as athletes but as leaders. They were both high-caliber players from nearby West Tennessee high schools. They took time to teach me, pulling me aside to explain reads, spacing, and the little things that made a big difference. They didn't have to, but they took the time to help me understand the intricacies of the game at a higher level. I absorbed everything I could.

But then came the curveball.

During a routine athletic physical, my blood pressure was high. The doctor suggested follow-up tests. A few weeks later, an EKG revealed an irregularity. The doctor came into the room with an uneasy look on her face as she explained that the EKG results showed something concerning about my heart. She didn't know exactly what was wrong, but she emphasized that it needed to be addressed immediately.

I was referred to a heart specialist in Jackson, Tennessee, that afternoon. As we drove over, I could feel my nervousness building with every passing mile. I kept trying to tell myself it was probably nothing, that maybe the EKG had just picked up a fluke. But the unknowns were heavy. What if it was serious? Would this change everything?

A thought crossed my mind, something that hadn't seemed relevant until now. My twin sister, Natalie, was born with a hole in her heart. It was something that had healed naturally over time without ever causing her any real issues. But with us being twins, I couldn't help but wonder if I might have something similar—something that had gone

CONFRONTING THE UNEXPECTED

undetected all these years. It was strange to think that, after all the physicals, all the training, and all the years playing sports, there could be something wrong inside me that no one had noticed until now.

After numerous tests, monitors, and time spent running on a treadmill, the diagnosis was Wolff-Parkinson-White syndrome (WPW). This rare heart condition causes an irregular or abnormally fast heartbeat, known as an arrhythmia. The doctor said it occurs when a person is born with an extra electrical pathway in their heart, which can cause rapid heartbeats. But he seemed calm about it, reassuring us that I should be fine, that there were no immediate concerns, and that I could continue with my normal activities.

So, he cleared me to continue my normal activities but urged caution and monitoring. Our family physician, who had received the report from the heart specialist's office, called Mom. Her tone was more cautious, emphasizing that if I experienced any symptoms like tightness or pain in my chest, dizziness, lightheadedness, fainting, palpitations, or shortness of breath, we should call her immediately. Mom assured her that we would, but as we continued down the road, I could feel the weight of her concern filling the car.

I brushed it off…until…

One quiet night, several weeks later, I snuck into the gym for extra shots. Mid-workout, a sharp pain shot through my chest. I dropped to one knee, remembering the doctor's warning. As the pain faded, I went straight home and told my parents. My mom didn't leave my side that night, and by morning, she had me scheduled with a top cardiologist at Vanderbilt Children's Hospital: Dr. Frank Fish.

Dr. Fish ran his own tests and confirmed the diagnosis. Calm but direct, he explained the condition and laid out the plan: a cardiac ablation. It wasn't open-heart surgery. It was a catheter procedure to eliminate the extra electrical pathway. Still, the word "procedure" shook me. He explained that while the risk was small, not addressing WPW carried a bigger one: sudden cardiac arrest.

Mom asked about the timing of the procedure, mentioning that school was set to start the following week. He scheduled the procedure for that Friday. He could perform the procedure that morning, and I'd only need to stay overnight for observation, meaning I could head home Saturday morning. The thought of such a life-altering procedure happening so soon was overwhelming, but knowing the timeline gave me a sense of relief.

We left the farm before dawn. Mom and Natalie made the trip with me. My grandmother also met us at the hospital coming from Memphis. George was down in Tampa, continuing his own journey in college, and Dad stayed behind for work, as I had assured him everything would be fine and that there was nowhere comfortable for them to stay overnight anyway.

As I lay strapped to the cold operating table, arms stretched out and music playing through speakers, I cracked a smile. "Whatever gets you ready, crank it up," I thought. A nurse leaned in and asked if I was ready.

"Yes, ma'am," I said. "Let's do this."

I took a deep breath. The nurse administered the anesthesia, and the room faded away into darkness.

CHAPTER 12

Against the Clock: Rising Through the Challenge

"You don't inspire your teammates by showing them how amazing you are. You inspire them by showing them how amazing they are."
Robyn Benincasa

Waking up from surgery, I thought I'd only been out for half an hour. "That didn't take too long," I mumbled to Dr. Fish. He laughed. "It took almost six hours," he said. Fatigue settled into my body, confirming the truth.

Next came a shot of adenosine to confirm that the extra heart pathway had been destroyed. "You won't be able to breathe for a few seconds," Dr. Fish warned. "It'll feel like an elephant is sitting on your chest—but only for 10 seconds." That sounded harmless enough—until the shot hit. The pressure was suffocating. My lungs refused to work. Ten seconds stretched into eternity before air rushed back in. I gasped, shaken but relieved.

Dr. Fish smiled. "That's what we wanted. Your heart's fixed."

The next morning, after a restless night in the hospital, we were discharged. Bruising from the catheter showed up as expected—huge blotches on my neck and groin—but I didn't care. All I could think about was getting back to the court and making the most of my senior year. The time I'd lost recovering from this ordeal couldn't hold me back any longer.

The dream of playing college ball still burned, though Memphis was looking less likely. I knew the kind of players recruited at that level were already well into their recruitment journeys. The calls and the letters weren't coming for me. I hadn't drawn the attention of D1 programs, but I still had a shot. Individually, I had to show that I was a player worth investing in. More importantly, our team had to win, and not just in the regular season. We had to go deep into the postseason. We needed to make a run to the state tournament.

The pressure was on, but after everything I had been through, I felt ready to face whatever challenges came my way. It was time to put my head back down, get to work, and chase the dream with everything I had left.

Our season started strong. We suffered only one loss early in the season—an upset that lit a fire under us. We bounced back with dominant wins, including against tougher Double-A and Triple-A opponents. One of the season's most unforgettable moments came during our rivalry game at McNairy Central's "Roundhouse."

Both teams came into the game with nearly identical records—seven or eight wins apiece and only one loss. McNairy Central came out firing on all cylinders, quickly jumping to a commanding lead. Down twenty at the half, and as the captain and leader, I stood up; I rallied the team with a speech straight from the heart. "This isn't the end; it's just the moment we prove who we are. Champions aren't defined by how they play when it's easy—they're made in moments like this, when everything is on the line. Look around! This is your family! We don't give up on family, and we don't give up on ourselves. Let's go out there and take what we deserve!"

The locker room erupted with energy. We charged back onto the court with a renewed sense of purpose. The McNairy Central players, who had seemed confident and dominant moments ago, now wore expressions of worry. They had underestimated us, thinking the game was already won. But the tide was about to turn.

We played with a tenacity and focus that had been absent in the first half. Stop by stop, bucket by bucket, we chipped away at their lead. We clawed back, possession by possession.

AGAINST THE CLOCK: RISING THROUGH THE CHALLENGE

In all my years of playing, I had never been the one to hit the game-winning shot. My role had always been to set up my teammates, to create opportunities for others to shine. But in this moment, I knew that if I wanted to be the difference-maker, it had to start with my defense. The player I was guarding made a spin move, leaving the ball exposed for just a moment. I seized the opportunity, swiping the ball cleanly from him.

The gym erupted. I took two hard dribbles down the court and laid the ball up, giving us a one-point lead with just eight seconds left on the clock. The roar of our fans was deafening, and adrenaline surged through me. But the game wasn't over yet. We still needed one last defensive stand.

McNairy Central put the ball in the hands of their best player, Ross Shelton. It seemed like he was about to seal the game with a layup, but our defense collapsed on him, forcing him to make a tough, last-second pass to a teammate. It was a brilliant pass, the kind only a player of his caliber could make. But as the ball hit his teammate's hands, it slipped through his fingers and rolled out of bounds as the buzzer sounded.

We won by one, sealing a comeback for the ages. That night taught me something I'd carry with me forever: in life, you're never truly out of it as long as you're willing to fight, believe in yourself, and trust the people around you.

We never got our rematch in our home gym—they canceled the return game due to rain—but we kept our focus. Then came Middleton.

We faced them to close the regular season and suffered a tough loss. The game was being played on their court, and we knew the atmosphere was going to be electric. But we came out with flat energy, missed opportunities, and a gym full of momentum we couldn't match. When we met them again in the district tournament, we were hungry for revenge. But Middleton humbled us again—on their home floor. That second loss stung worse than the first.

Our coaches pushed us hard the following week. Practices were brutal, but necessary. By the time regionals arrived, we were reborn—firing on all cylinders. We breezed through the quarterfinals and semifinals, setting up another showdown with Middleton in the region title game.

This time, we were ready. This would be the fourth match-up with them that season. We dominated from start to finish and finally got our redemption. I was honored with another All-Region selection, but the trophy meant more. We were champions again.

Up next was the new Sectional Tournament at UT Martin—win and you're in the state tournament. With a first-round bye, we played Greenfield in the semifinal. Early on, we played tight and out of sync. Our best player wasn't being aggressive, despite having a mismatch. I took charge.

During a timeout, I looked him in the eyes and said in front of the whole team and coaches, "He can't guard you. Get in the post. Go to work."

Coach nodded. "You heard him."

From there, the game flipped. Our best player dominated, and we won the game. For me, it was a defining moment as a leader, knowing that my voice and confidence in my teammate had helped spark the turnaround. That win punched our ticket to state. We followed it with a statement victory over South Fulton, claiming the first-ever West Tennessee Class A Sectional championship.

That title meant everything. It was a testament to the resilience and growth of our team. The format would only last two years, but we were the first. A team that had grown through heartbreak, surgery, setbacks, and rivalry losses had now made history.

We were going to the state tournament—cementing our place in school history.

CHAPTER 13

Moments That Shape a Legacy

"Every closed door is a chance to find another way in."
Root

The several days leading up to the state tournament felt like the longest stretch of my life. Our practices were intense, fueled by momentum and purpose, but two of our best players had fallen ill—one even had to be hospitalized. They were eventually cleared to play, but they weren't at full strength. Even so, their determination inspired us all.

As game day neared, it felt like the whole town shut down. Nearly every business, teacher, and family made the trip to Murfreesboro to support us at Middle Tennessee State University. It wasn't just about basketball anymore—it was about community. We carried the pride and hopes of everyone who had stood with us.

Walking into the arena was surreal. I couldn't help but think of Matt and Bubba, who had led our school to the state championship game four years earlier. Now, it was our turn. I wasn't just chasing the appearance; I wanted the gold ball.

We opened against Moore County, the top-ranked team all season. But they had stumbled in their Sectional Championship, and we saw a crack. Quietly, we knew that whoever won this game would likely win it all.

We came out firing, jumping to a 6-0 lead. Then I made a steal and saw our best player trailing me. Without hesitation, I flipped the ball back, expecting the kind of momentum-shifting dunk we'd executed all season. But he missed it. Moore County scored easily in transition, and just like that, the game's rhythm shifted.

Should I have just taken the layup? Maybe. But I trusted him. That's what teammates do.

From there, Moore County took control. We went into halftime down 26-15—our lowest scoring half of the year. In the locker room, our coach reminded us of who we were, and we came out swinging.

We clawed back into it, possession by possession. But Moore County was too strong, especially with two of our guys still battling illnesses. We ran out of time, falling 61-47.

I played every second until the final two minutes. When Coach subbed me out, I began the long walk to the bench, and I broke. The tears came freely. This game, this journey—it had been everything to me—basketball was my passion, my purpose, my life. And now, in an instant, it was over.

As the final buzzer sounded, I gathered my emotions enough to congratulate the players from Moore County. Then, I made my way to the locker room. I hugged teammates I had spent years battling, especially the seniors, Jay Rickman, Tyrone Luster, and Chris Smith. We didn't get the ending we wanted, but we had written a story worth remembering.

The ride home was quiet, heavy with reflection. The championship dream that we had chased all season was now just a memory, and the reality of the final buzzer echoed in my mind. I still had soccer coming up, but it wasn't the same. Basketball was my heartbeat. And now? Now there were no scholarship offers. I wasn't on anyone's radar.

Averaging 9 points and 5 assists. Solid stats for my role—but not flashy enough to turn heads.

I could feel the dream slipping away.

Mom reminded me, "Don't measure your story by this one chapter." Her words stayed with me. I wasn't ready to give up.

So, I got to work. I created highlight tapes, compiled statistics, and sent letters to every junior college and NAIA program I could locate.

MOMENTS THAT SHAPE A LEGACY

Soccer season came at the perfect time. After the sting of not receiving any basketball scholarship offers, it was a welcome escape—something that let me compete without pressure, just for the love of the game. For the first time since my sophomore year, I was finally moved out of the goalie position and placed at forward, the role I had wanted all along.

It changed everything.

Suddenly, I was scoring in nearly every game. With each goal, our confidence soared. We climbed to the top of the district standings, and for the first time in our program's short history, we became the team to beat.

The recognition started pouring in—more than I'd ever received for basketball. People began to wonder if I was better at soccer than the sport I had given everything to for years. As proud as I was, the success was bittersweet. I still loved basketball more.

Still, the season was unforgettable. We won the district and region titles, and I was named MVP of both tournaments. We entered the state tournament as underdogs, and although we were knocked out in the first round, just making it there in our third year of the program was an achievement in itself. I finished the season as the school's all-time leader in goals for both a season and a career.

I was proud, but soccer would never replace basketball in my heart. I knew I wasn't done chasing that dream. I still had unfinished business on the hardwood.

I started signing up for unsigned senior showcases. One was in Georgetown, Kentucky, and since Dad couldn't make the trip, Mom took me.

The gym was packed. The competition was tough. But I played maybe the best game of my life—18 points, nearly 10 assists. I controlled the tempo, made smart plays, and defended hard. I felt sure someone would talk to me afterward.

But no one did.

The ride home was long. Mom tried to encourage me, but I couldn't hide the hurt. I felt invisible. Still, I told myself, there's one more showcase.

That one was at Union University, where Matt, Bubba, Gaylon, and Steve had played. I played well, but not as well as I had in Georgetown. Still, I hoped.

Again—no offers. No conversations.

To make matters harder, one of my high school teammates signed to a junior college. I was happy for him, but I couldn't help feeling like I'd been overlooked.

I would've signed anywhere—on the moon, if someone had asked. I just wanted to play.

That summer, I returned to Union for pickup games, just as I had before. But this time, it felt different. With high school behind me, my parents gave me more freedom. I stayed overnight on campus, played until late, and started forming deeper bonds with the college guys.

One of the first new players I met was Enelio Moreno. At 6'6" and 280 pounds, he was a force—but off the court, he was gentle, joyful, and humble. He became a good friend. Many years later, I'd watch his sons become stars—Michael, who broke records at EKU, and Malachi, who became a McDonald's All-American and signed with Kentucky.

After games, we'd all hang out at Matt's apartment. It wasn't just basketball guys. That's where I met Blake Allen and Eric Olexa, two baseball players at Union. Up until then, most of my friendships had been basketball-centric. But Blake and Eric helped me see how athletes across sports share the same grind—the same mental battles, discipline, and emotional highs and lows.

Those nights were filled with stories, laughter, and camaraderie. They reminded me that no matter what sport we played, we were all chasing something—connection, purpose, excellence.

I didn't know if basketball would ever offer me another shot, but I knew this: I wasn't alone. I had people in my corner, a story worth telling, and a drive that wouldn't let me quit.

That summer didn't bring a scholarship. But it brought something just as valuable—clarity, connection, and lifelong friendships.

CHAPTER 14

The Road to Memphis

*"Dreams don't wait for perfect circumstances—
they demand relentless pursuit and unshakable faith."*
ROOT

As summer wore on, I found myself back on the job site with Dad, trying to earn a little money before heading to college. I had been accepted to Memphis, and unless a last-minute basketball scholarship came through, that's where I'd be. Still, I felt defeated. I wasn't myself—dragging, distracted, weighed down by the sense that I had failed.

One day, while working with Dad and his friend James Dennie, they finally asked me what was wrong. I hesitated, then admitted the truth: "I feel like a failure. I wasn't good enough to keep playing basketball."

Without missing a beat, James asked, "Where would you want to play if you could pick anywhere?"

"Memphis," I said without hesitation.

Dad jumped in. "You've already been accepted there. Enroll in classes. Walk on."

Just like that, everything snapped into focus. Their simple advice gave me clarity: if Memphis was still the dream, and no other school had come calling, then the path forward was clear—I just had to fight for it and keep chasing it. The dream wasn't dead—it just required a different path. That moment lit a fire inside me again.

ROOT

With the decision made, I now had a plan, and for the first time in a while, I felt 100 percent confident that I was going to achieve my goal. The summer had been a rollercoaster of emotions, but now I was focused. Memphis was the destination, and nothing was going to stop me from making my dream a reality.

Later that summer, as I stepped out of the local gas station, holding a cold Gatorade in one hand and heading back to my truck, I ran into a man who had supported our high school team for years. He rolled his window down, a friendly smile on his face, and leaned out slightly. "What are you going to do for basketball this season?" he asked casually.

Without hesitation, I responded, "I'm going to Memphis. I'm going to try to walk on the team."

For a moment, I expected encouragement, maybe even excitement at my ambition. Instead, his smile turned into a sarcastic grin. His voice took on a condescending tone as he replied, "Good luck with that. You're the wrong type of player to be on that team."

As he drove off, his words had hit me hard, but they also fueled me. Who was he to judge what I could or couldn't do? That interaction pushed me to prove him wrong. One thought consumed my mind: *I will show him.* This wasn't just about proving it to myself anymore; it was about proving everyone wrong who had ever doubted me.

I needed perspective, so I went straight to see Roger D. Hill, a longtime mentor and retired Army Lieutenant Colonel. Over the years, he had become someone I could always count on, always ready with wisdom and advice, and always pushing me to see beyond the borders of our small town.

When I arrived, he was standing inside his kitchen by the island—a familiar spot where we'd shared countless conversations. As I stepped into the room, he looked up, and in an instant, he knew something was wrong.

When I told him what the man had said, Roger didn't flinch. He spoke with the kind of stern yet encouraging voice only he could muster.

THE ROAD TO MEMPHIS

"You have everything you need to make your dreams a reality," he told me. "The road to success isn't always easy, but it's always worth it. Your belief in yourself is your greatest weapon."

That was all I needed to hear. I wasn't going to let anyone else's doubts define me. My dream was mine to chase.

Mid-August arrived, and it was time to leave for college. Excitement and nerves churned inside me as I thought about the next chapter of my life. At the same time, there was a bittersweetness to it all. Natalie, my twin, was heading to Loyola in New Orleans—six hours from home. It was the first time we'd ever really been apart. For the first time, we would be living in separate cities, each chasing our dreams. I asked Mom and Dad to focus on getting her settled. Memphis was just two hours away, and I'd be fine.

With help from Edna Nelson, one of Mom's best friends who worked at the university, I was placed in Robinson Hall—a quieter dorm that gave me space to focus. She was a guiding hand for me in navigating the campus logistics. My small-town world was behind me. Ahead was a new challenge: walk on to the Memphis basketball team and prove I belonged.

A few days into classes, I ran into Andreus "Dre" Shannon at the Richardson Towers cafeteria. Dre, a year older, had been a high school rival at Hardin County. It felt good to see a familiar face. When I told him about trying out for the team, he encouraged me—and then told me where the real competition was.

"If you're serious, you need to go to the Elma Roane Fieldhouse. Monday through Thursday, that's where the best ballers are. I'll warn you, though, you're probably going to be the only white guy in there."

Being the only white guy on the court wasn't something that ever fazed me. The only thing that mattered to me was the opportunity to play against better competition, to push myself and prove that I belonged.

That afternoon, I went.

I arrived early, the gym almost empty, with just a few guys shooting around. I took my place at one of the baskets and started warming up.

Gradually, more players trickled in, the gym coming alive with the sound of bouncing basketballs and chatter. I could feel the intensity growing, a quiet competitiveness hanging in the air.

At first, nobody picked me. It stung a little—I was shooting well, hitting nearly everything I put up—but I understood. I was the new guy, an unfamiliar face, and I needed to prove myself before anyone would take a chance on me.

I kept shooting. Dre eventually called next and waved me over to join his team. This was it—my shot to prove myself.

The rules were simple: first to seven wins, one-point baskets, call your own fouls. Winners stay.

As we stepped onto the court, I could feel eyes on me, measuring me up, waiting to see if I could hold my own.

I locked in—quickly settling into a rhythm, playing defense, making smart passes, and hitting shots. We won, and I stayed on the court. Game after game, I earned my place.

During one of the games, someone yelled out, "Y'all better guard that white boy. He can shoot!"

By day's end, I was no longer a question mark. I was a regular.

That small gym inside the Elma Roane Fieldhouse became my battleground. Every afternoon, I showed up—grinding, improving, preparing for tryouts.

Around the same time, I decided to join a fraternity. After meeting the brothers of Sigma Phi Epsilon—SigEp—I knew I'd found my place. Guys like Tony Martin, Scott Bendure, Michael Redus, James Rudolph, Stephen Fuller, Justin Larrabee, Justin Atkins, Jamie West, David Jackson, my Big Brother Levi Gay, and many others quickly became more than friends. They were a support system.

They understood that basketball was my top priority—that making the team was my dream and that it would require a great deal of my time and focus. But instead of viewing that as a problem, they reassured me that my goals mattered. They made it clear they'd find a way to keep me as a brother, no matter how demanding my schedule became. Their unwavering support only strengthened my decision to pledge Sig Ep, and in that moment, I knew I had made the right choice.

The summer of reflection, hard work, and rediscovery finally gave way to a sense of purpose that I had been searching for all along. Now I had a plan, a community, and a purpose. Memphis wasn't just a city anymore—it was the next chapter of the dream.

CHAPTER 15

Welcome to the Jungle

*"Success is not final, failure is not fatal:
It is the courage to continue that counts."*
WINSTON S. CHURCHILL

The crisp October air buzzed with anticipation as I made my way to the Elma Roane Fieldhouse for basketball tryouts. The gym, home to the women's team, seated about 2,800 but felt massive that night, packed with energy and expectation. Around 50 guys gathered, shooting and talking, all hoping to wear a Memphis Tigers uniform. I was the only white guy trying out, something I was used to by now, but the diversity still stood out. Most of the guys were local—guys I'd been playing pickup with all semester. We shared the same dream: to play for the Tigers.

Several hundred students filled the stands, curious to see who might make the cut. Coaches and managers moved around, organizing us into teams of four. I got paired with a 6'8" guy I recognized from pickup. He was a force—skilled, powerful, and a familiar sight at the gym.

I wore a navy-blue sleeveless shirt from a senior showcase and white Nike shorts. On my feet were my Air Penny 1s, a quiet nod to the Memphis legend himself. It felt right, like a moment I'd been waiting for.

The rules were simple:

- Half-court games.
- Call your own fouls.

- Every shot made counts as one point.
- First team to three buckets wins.
- Winners stay on the court.
- Simple enough.
- No coaches interfering. Just hoop.

We were at the end of the arena without bleachers behind the basket, which somehow made the space feel more intimate. Glaring down at us from the wall behind, a massive set of fierce, blue tiger eyes decorated with the words "Welcome to the Jungle" sent a shiver down my spine, a constant reminder of the intensity and challenge that lay ahead.

The first two teams started, and I watched with a mix of anxiety and readiness. My turn came quickly.

We started on defense. After a quick bucket by the other team, we got the ball. I fed the big guy with a sharp bounce pass—bucket. On the next possession, another dish from me, another score. We were up 2-1. One stop later, the big man kicked it out to me at the top of the key. I launched it. The ball soared through the air, the crowd holding their breath, and then it swished through the net. Game over.

"If they keep doubling me," he said, "I'll keep kicking it to you."

"You keep doing that," I replied, "I'll keep knocking them down."

That's exactly what happened. We rattled off win after win—seven or eight in a row. The crowd started gathering around our end of the court, cheering louder every game. I hit 11 or 12 shots in a row at one point. "That white boy ain't missin'!" someone shouted. The energy was electric. The crowd's energy was felt. Their chants and cheers for me were deafening; each shot was greeted with a collective "Ooohhh," and every swish was met with an ecstatic "Ewww."

I looked across the gym and saw the assistant coaches huddled up at half court, watching us intently. It felt like everything I had worked for had led to this moment. I'd always admired the great shooters in our program's history—Russ, Seth, Matt, Bubba, and Gibbs. I wasn't one of them in high school. My shooting had been streaky at best.

WELCOME TO THE JUNGLE

But the summer after my senior year, I committed to changing that. Hundreds of shots every day. Footwork. Form. Focus. And now, when it mattered most, all that work paid off.

In that moment, under those circumstances, everything fell perfectly into place for me, so I seized my shot.

After an hour and a half, the coaches called everyone to center court and read out 10 names. I was one of them.

That night, I sprinted back to my dorm and called home. "I made the first cut!" I shouted when Mom answered. Her excitement matched mine. Dad got on the phone and told me how proud he was. I called George and Natalie next. My brother celebrated like he'd made the team himself. My sister, always my biggest supporter, was thrilled. That moment, sharing the news with them, made it even more real. Then I called Bubba. He answered right away, and when I told him the news, he let out one of those signature Bubba moments—loud, proud, and full of heart. "That's what I'm talking about!" he said. "You keep pushing, man. You will make it." Hearing that from him meant the world to me.

Thursday's final tryout was closed to the public—probably because of how rowdy the crowd had been on Tuesday. The gym felt more serious. And to make it tougher, the big guy I'd thrived with wasn't on my team this time. We played five-on-five, full court. First to seven. Every point mattered.

I played well—solid defense, smart passes—but I wasn't as dominant. Some guys hogged the ball, eager to show off. I stuck to my strengths: facilitating, playing team basketball. Looking back, maybe I should have been more aggressive. But that wasn't how I was wired. Coach Van taught me long ago to be a pass-first point guard, and those instincts were hard to shake.

The tryout ended, and they told us they'd call with a decision. Walking back to my dorm, I replayed every possession, wondering if I'd done enough.

Friday afternoon, the dorm phone rang. It was Coach Bill Pieczynski. He got right to it: they were keeping a guy who'd been practicing with the team already and a football player who'd join after the season. I hadn't made it.

I hung up, heart sinking. My dreams felt crushed. It felt like the air had been sucked from the room.

I sat in silence for a while, letting the disappointment wash over me. But even through the sting, I knew this wasn't the end. I had come too far to let this be the last chapter. I was not going to let this setback define me.

A few weeks later, the Tigers' home opener rolled around. I decided to go.

Walking into the Pyramid brought everything rushing back—a familiar feeling I had experienced before. I remembered that moment as a kid in junior high, walking through that same parking lot, dreaming of the day I'd play there back when we had made the trip to see the women's team play Tennessee. I remember looking up at the arena, feeling it deep in my soul: "This is where I belong."

Now, as I walked through those same doors, the feeling hadn't changed. If anything, it was stronger. Even though I didn't make the team, I wasn't done chasing that dream. I still believed I'd play here someday.

This wasn't a failure. It was a detour. I knew who I was, what I was capable of, and what I was willing to do to make my dream come true. The fire hadn't gone out. If anything, it was burning hotter than ever.

CHAPTER 16

Dealing with the Disappointment

"Be thankful for all the struggles you go through. They make you stronger, wiser, and humble. Don't let it break you. Let it make you."

Root

As my first semester at Memphis drew to a close, I kept returning to the Elma Roane Fieldhouse. I hadn't made the team, but I wasn't ready to let go. I kept playing pickup games, sharpening my skills, and clinging to the hope that I might earn a spot the following year. Each time I stepped onto the court, I pushed myself harder, working on my game with a relentless drive. The court became my sanctuary, a place where disappointment transformed into determination.

Getting cut hurt deeply, but I refused to let it define me. Instead of wallowing, I turned the sting of rejection into fuel. I worked harder, stayed focused, and reminded myself that success is often born from failure. The path to your dream isn't always straight, but the detours teach you resilience.

At the same time, I was becoming a full-fledged member of Sigma Phi Epsilon. The brotherhood I found in SigEp became an anchor. They didn't see me as a guy who didn't make the team—they saw me as a brother, someone worth rooting for. Whether we were hanging out at the house, studying late into the night, or just grabbing a bite to eat, they reminded me there was more to college than basketball. And yet, basketball remained central to who I was.

What I didn't know then was that those same fraternity brothers would soon become my biggest fans. They were always the first in line on game days, filling the front rows of the Pyramid with their voices. They didn't just cheer—they roared. It was them who started the now-infamous chant that would follow me every time I stepped on the court: "ROOOOT!" What began as a playful cheer to try and get me into a game quickly spread through the student section and eventually the entire arena.

Their belief in me was louder than any doubt I ever carried. It helped define my college experience and eventually became part of my identity on the court.

While I found community in SigEp and purpose in basketball, my academics began to slip. I was taking 12 credit hours—just four classes—and by semester's end, I had earned two A's and two F's. A 2.0 GPA. Not failing, but barely staying eligible. Truthfully, I hadn't even thought about eligibility requirements. I was too wrapped up in pickup games, fraternity life, and chasing my hoop dreams.

The realization that I had to go home and face my parents with bad grades sat heavily on my chest. I dreaded the conversation. They were always supportive, especially when it came to basketball, but this felt different. Academic performance had always mattered in our house, and I knew they'd be disappointed.

So, I waited.

I didn't say anything until after Christmas and New Year's. I let us enjoy the holidays as a family—kept the mood light, helped with chores, and celebrated traditions. But when the time came, I sat them down in the living room of our farmhouse. The fire crackled in the background, casting warm shadows on the walls, but the room felt tighter than usual.

"I made a 2.0," I said.

I braced for anger or disappointment, but it didn't come—not the way I expected. Sure, they gave me a firm talk about priorities and responsibilities. But their response was measured. They told me they'd talk in private about what I needed and how they could help. That shocked me, honestly. But in hindsight, I understand why. They

DEALING WITH THE DISAPPOINTMENT

weren't just raising a basketball player. They were raising someone who knew how to fight through failure.

Their support was exactly what I needed. My parents knew that success is not the absence of failure; it's the persistence through failure. In the days that followed, we had several meaningful conversations—some while hunting in the deer stand with Dad, others while cleaning up the barn or putting away decorations with Mom. They never yelled. They offered wisdom. Encouragement. Perspective.

One night, while watching Memphis play Arkansas, the fire crackling, my parents reminded me plainly: "If you want to ever step on that floor as a Tiger, your grades have to come first. Coaches won't waste their time on a walk-on who can't stay eligible."

It was the wake-up call I needed. I'd been focused solely on my game—getting stronger, faster, more confident. But none of that would matter if I couldn't stay on the court because of grades.

That night shifted everything for me.

I returned to campus with a new focus. Basketball still mattered, but so did the books. I promised myself I wouldn't just chase the dream—I'd do it right. I'd take care of my business in the classroom and keep working on the court, because both were necessary to achieve my goals.

By mid-January, it was time to head back to Memphis for my second semester. The winter air bit at my skin as I packed the last of my things. The farm, quiet and calm beneath the pale afternoon sky, was as beautiful as ever—but I knew it was time. I was going back with a new mindset. The month away had given me time to reflect, to reset, and to map out how I'd attack this semester: with discipline, with focus, and with a hunger to get things right, especially in the classroom.

I waited until Sunday, January 9th, to return—just in time to settle in before Monday classes began. I wanted to make sure I was as prepared as possible. My roommate, Trey, had already unpacked when I walked in. We caught up on our breaks, swapped stories, and talked about what we hoped to get out of the new semester, but soon it was time to turn in. I wanted to get a good night's sleep, to wake up fresh and ready to take on the new semester with focus and determination. I felt a quiet confidence growing within me, knowing that this semester would be different. I was locked in.

Monday morning was frigid, the kind of cold that makes everyone walk a little faster with their heads down. Campus was buzzing but quiet, in that first-day-of-classes kind of way. My schedule had all my classes wrapped up by noon, on purpose. I knew I'd need afternoons free. Since I wasn't on the team, it was time to look for a job, and I wanted the flexibility.

That first day was mostly syllabi and introductions. Nothing too heavy. I looked around each classroom, curious who might become a study partner or a new friend. I still loved being social, but now I was trying to balance that with purpose. After class, I headed to the University Center to grab lunch. The line was long, students packed in, and they were swapping holiday stories. It felt good to be back in the flow of campus life. With food in hand, I headed back to my dorm, ready to finalize my game plan for the semester—daily study time, shooting sessions, workouts, and a job search.

But as I opened the door, I knew something was off.

Trey looked stunned. Not just surprised—stunned. He told me someone had called and left a message. "Some coach… Pieczynski? From the basketball team." My heart jumped. Coach Pieczynski? The same coach who had been at the tryouts when I didn't make the cut?

Trey hit play on the answering machine.

"Hello, this message is for Nathaniel Root. I'd like to discuss the possibility of you coming to practice with the basketball team this semester. Please come by the basketball offices located in the athletics building when you receive this message."

I stood there, frozen. He wanted to talk to me about joining the team? Then everything hit me at once—hope, disbelief, nerves. I scarfed down my lunch without tasting it, grabbed my coat, and made a beeline for the athletic office.

The cold January wind didn't even register. I walked across campus

DEALING WITH THE DISAPPOINTMENT

on adrenaline alone. When I stepped into the athletics building and rode the elevator to the second floor, my heart thumped like a bass drum.

Chitra Rampersad, the men's basketball secretary, greeted me with a smile. "I was wondering how long it would take you to get here," she said. I smiled, still trying to wrap my head around it all.

"As soon as I heard the message, I came straight here," I replied, out of breath.

She led me down the hall to Coach Pieczynski's office. He and Coach Rike were waiting. Their tone was friendly but serious. They explained that a football player named Ryan Johnson, who had walked on after his season, had decided to return to football full-time, opening up a spot.

They didn't sugarcoat anything. I wouldn't be guaranteed a jersey or playing time. I might never dress out. But if I were willing to give my all—arrive early, stay late, be a great teammate—I could join as a practice player. There was one condition: I had to pass through the NCAA Clearinghouse.

The reality of the situation started to sink in, and despite the uncertainty, I felt a surge of determination. This was my chance to prove myself, to earn my place on the team, even if it was just as a practice player.

My response was instant: "Yes. I'll do whatever it takes."

They both smiled, stood up, and shook my hand. "Congratulations," they said. "You're officially a Memphis Tiger."

Those words hit me like a lightning bolt. Every hour in the gym, every moment of doubt, and every setback had all led to this. I was finally getting my opportunity.

Coach Cal and Root

Root, Junior Year at Memphis

Root, Senior Year at Memphis

Root and Shannon Forman, Sophomore Year

Root, Sophomore Year

Root in high school

Memphis Seniors 2003—Earl Barron, John Grice, Root, and Chris Massie

2001–2002 Memphis Team

The Root Family

Root and Uncle Ned Plunk

George III, Root, and Natalie

Matt Hoover and Daddy Root

Root and Fr. Hood

Momma Root and Earl Barron

Courtney Trask and Root

Root and Erin

Root, Earl Barron, J White, and Jeremy Hunt

Rhamen, Rob, Earl, Bubba, Root, Gaylon, and Doug

Gaylon, Root, and Duane

Rob Bullington, Root, Lamont Robinson, Russ Kennamore, and JT Livezey

Erin Root, Lena Taylor, Root, and Maddie Kirk

Earl, Aimee Riser, Natalie, and Root at a BBBS Conf.

Michael Moreno, Malachi Moreno, Root, Enelio Moreno, Steve Poindexter, Gaylon Moore, and Bubba Hoover

CHAPTER 17

The Start of Something Big

"Sometimes you wait so long for a moment, you start to wonder if it will ever come. And then, when it does—it hits you all at once."

Root

Once Coach P and Coach Rike welcomed me aboard, they sent me to meet with an associate athletic director to handle the NCAA eligibility paperwork. The nerves hit again—I had a 2.0 GPA, barely the minimum to stay eligible. But to my relief, it was enough.

Lunetha Pryor, who served as the assistant to Head Coach Johnny Jones, played a pivotal role in helping me officially join the team. She personally took me to the compliance office and made sure every detail of my NCAA Clearinghouse paperwork was completed. Without her guidance and persistence behind the scenes, my dream of becoming a Memphis Tiger might never have come to life. I'll always be grateful for her belief in me and her quiet but powerful support.

After I completed all of the necessary paperwork, I sprinted back to my dorm and started calling everyone: Mom and Dad first—both proud as could be. George and Natalie were next, and their reactions made it even more real. One call after another—to Bubba, Matt, Russ, Rob, Lamont, Doug, and J.T.—I got to relive the moment, sharing the news with some of the very people who had helped shape my journey. The celebration was short-lived, though, because I had to wait a few days before getting cleared by the NCAA.

Each day felt like a month. I'd wake up, check my phone, and hear nothing. Just silence. Until finally, on January 25th, 2000, Coach P called. I was officially eligible. They had a home game against UAB the next day, and while I wasn't needed for practice yet, he had tickets waiting so I could sit behind the bench.

Game day came, and I arrived at the Pyramid early. Sitting that close to the action, watching everything from a player's perspective, was surreal. We won 84–70. Coach P caught up with me afterward and said, "Be here at the Pyramid tomorrow at 3:30 pm for practice." That was it. My moment had arrived.

The next day, my classes felt like background noise. I couldn't focus. All I could think about was the court. Another walk-on, who lived down the hall from me in the same dorm, rode down with me. He cracked jokes the whole ride, trying to calm my nerves, and it helped—a little.

When we pulled into the back lot at the Pyramid, it all hit me. This was real. Walking through the back entrance and into the depths of the halls, we made our way to the locker room on the opposite side. Inside, the University of Memphis logo lit up the waiting area like a beacon. I turned right and entered the locker room—and it stopped me cold. It was spotless, massive, and fully outfitted. Nothing like the cramped, dusty lockers from high school.

Carl Rosen, one of the managers, greeted me and showed me to my locker. Everything I needed was there: jerseys, socks, shoes, compression gear, headbands—you name it. I remember thinking how different this was from high school, where you had to bring all your own gear and hope you didn't forget something essential. Here, everything was prepared and waiting. That's when I saw my practice jersey: number 4. Not my first choice, but I didn't care. I had a locker. I had a number. I was part of the team.

Ray Burr, the team trainer, came by and introduced himself and explained that every player was required to have their ankles either taped or wear ankle braces—a team requirement. I'd never had issues with them before, but I trusted him. Ray had that calming presence, the kind that steadied you even when your heart was racing. He treated me like I'd been there all season.

THE START OF SOMETHING BIG

Back in the locker room, I pulled on the gear and started lacing up. Two players walked over—Keiron Shine and Marcus Moody, both Memphis natives and team leaders. Keiron broke the ice: "You play the one or the two?" referring to the basketball positions. I told him I played the one in high school but could slide to the two. Keiron grinned at Marcus and said, "Told you—he's giving me breaks in practice."

It was their way of welcoming me, and it worked. I relaxed. I couldn't help but laugh to myself. Apparently, they had been debating over who would get more rest now that the new guy had arrived. Maybe I could fit in here after all.

I jogged out to the court, adrenaline spiking. The Pyramid felt impossibly huge—20,000+ seats, 32 stories tall. I looked around and imagined the legends who had played here: Penny Hardaway, David Vaughn, Lorenzen Wright, and so many others. Now it was my turn to leave a mark.

As I stepped onto the court, I paused, looking straight up, and said, "God, thank you." I started warming up, and one by one, my teammates introduced themselves. The first was Courtney Trask. He and I clicked instantly. Although we came from different places—he from Baton Rouge and I from rural Tennessee—we connected on a level that would evolve into a lifelong brotherhood. He was one of the first to make me feel like I truly belonged.

Practice started, and Coach Johnny Jones huddled us up. He wasn't just a coach—he was a leader, a mentor, a man who genuinely cared. Thrust into the head coaching role at the beginning of the season, he had a lot on his shoulders. But you could tell the players respected him deeply.

As drills began, reality hit hard. I was out of shape. Pickup games hadn't prepared me for this level of intensity. My lungs burned, and my legs wobbled; my conditioning wasn't where it needed to be. Still, the guys encouraged me. No one mocked me or looked down on me. They pulled me along, cheered me on, and helped me push through.

This wasn't high school anymore. These were real players—Division

I athletes. The skill level was unreal. Watching Memphis games on TV, I always thought I could hang with these guys. TV didn't do them justice. But I wasn't intimidated. I was motivated, knowing I had to get better quickly.

After practice, I stayed behind to get extra shots up. As I headed back to the locker room, I noticed the other walk-on had already left, so I knew I'd have the ride back to campus to reflect on my first day as a Tiger. I felt tired but determined.

As I was hanging up my gear, I suddenly felt a presence behind me. I turned around and looked up—way up. It was Earl Barron, our 7-foot center.

He looked down at me and asked, "You're Root, right?" I nodded. He smiled and asked if I could give him a ride back to campus. "Heck yeah," I said, trying to hide my shock that he even knew my name.

As we stepped out of the Pyramid, the cold breeze from the nearby Mississippi River hit us hard. Earl squeezed into my tiny 1991 Toyota lowrider, knees touching the dashboard. As we drove, the heater had just kicked in, and suddenly I smelled something awful.

"Did you fart?" I asked.

He grinned. "Yeah, my bad."

We both busted out laughing. It was the first of many moments that would bond us beyond basketball. That's how brotherhood starts sometimes—not with a grand gesture, but with a bad fart and a good laugh.

CHAPTER 18

The News

*"God's timing is perfect. Never early, never late.
It takes a little patience and a lot of faith."*
Root

The next morning, practice started early. The team was heading to Hattiesburg later that afternoon for a matchup with Southern Miss. My thoughts were a whirlwind—how do I prove I belong? How do I make the most out of this chance? I wasn't recruited. The coaches didn't know my story. All they had was a strong tryout impression. I had to work harder than ever to earn their trust and a permanent spot.

Practice was intense and focused. The guys were locked in, preparing for the road game. Afterward, they boarded the charter bus, and I stood there, watching them roll out. It stung a little. After only two practices, I already felt part of the team, and I wanted to be there. But I knew my time was coming; I just had to keep working.

That Saturday, the Tigers lost a heartbreaker to Southern Miss, 67-66. The sting was real. But the next few days brought a silver lining: a bye week. We had Sunday and Monday off before gearing up for the biggest game of the season—Louisville.

While the official practices paused, the grind didn't. Big Earl, Courtney, Shannon Forman, and I hit the gym to stay sharp. It was during one of those extra sessions that the reality hit me—without dressing out, I wouldn't be in the record books, and I wouldn't officially be considered a player. There'd be no stat line, no photo, no trace. I had to find a way to make it official. I had to earn a uniform.

Only nine games remained. My window was shrinking. I was determined to do whatever it took to become the first Division I basketball player from my high school.

Tuesday's practice brought a wave of excitement—it was our first day in the new Larry O. Finch Practice Center. Walking into that gym, named after a Memphis legend, was like stepping into history. The three full courts, the state-of-the-art weight room, the players' lounge—it all felt surreal. I was stepping into a program built on legacy, grit, and greatness.

Larry Finch was a Memphis legend. A standout guard from 1970 to 1973, he led the Tigers to the NCAA Tournament and earned first-team All-American honors. His impact on the court and legacy in the Memphis Tigers Hall of Fame helped shape the program for generations.

After his playing days were over, Finch returned to the university as head coach, guiding the team from 1986 to 1997. His coaching tenure was just as legendary. Under his leadership, the Tigers made four NCAA Tournament appearances, including a trip to the Elite Eight in 1992. His influence extended beyond wins and losses; he became a mentor and a figure of respect in the community, solidifying his status as a true Memphis basketball legend.

Walking into the Finch Center through a side door, I was instantly amazed by the sheer size of the facility. The massive expanse felt like a far cry from the shared high school gym I had come from. Ray, our trainer, greeted me first. "Come on, Root! Let's get you taped up before the others get here." I followed him into the training room, once again in awe of the professional setup.

The training room was filled with more equipment than I had ever seen—treatment tables, stim machines, heating pads, resistance bands, and everything else we needed to perform at the highest level. It was a far cry from the basic bags of ice we had relied on in high school. This was no longer small-town Tennessee; this was next-level athletics.

THE NEWS

Then I found my new locker—huge, pristine, and stocked with all the gear I needed. The oak lockers had a warm, polished finish, each with a pullout drawer below and plush, Memphis-blue vinyl seats. My name wasn't on the gold plate yet, but I knew it would be. I threw on my number 4 jersey and hit the court.

That day, I asked Keiron Shine for a one-on-one. He was a senior guard and a leader on the team. "Keiron, I need to get better, and fast. Let's play one-on-one." His face lit up with that big grin of his—Keiron was always smiling, always in a good mood.

"Let's go!" he replied.

He smoked me, but that wasn't the point. Every time we played, I got better. And Keiron? He didn't hold back—he sharpened me.

Practice was intense. So intense, in fact, that Big Earl shattered a backboard with a dunk while doing two-on-two post work. Coach Jones blew his whistle and motioned us over to the middle court for three-on-two, two-on-one transition drills.

Five minutes later, during one rep, Courtney Trask brought the ball up the floor, with Kelly Wise and me running the wings. Courtney dished the ball to me on the right, and as the bottom defender stepped out to guard me, I lobbed the ball high above the rim. Kelly soared in, catching the lob and slamming it home with force.

Another sharp crack echoed through the gym. This time, the backboard bolts gave way, causing the entire structure to slide down the pole it was mounted on. The backboard dropped from 10 feet to around 8 feet. We all stood there, stunned. In the span of just 10 to 15 minutes, we had managed to break two backboards. The team's sheer power and athleticism were on full display that day.

Coach Jones shook his head, laughed, and called it: "That's it, practice is over. Get out of here before we tear this place down on the first day!"

Even though practice was cut short, most of us stayed for extra reps. That was the culture—work when no one's watching. For me, the hustle had only just begun. I knew that my role on the team wasn't guaranteed, and I had to prove myself every single day.

ROOT

As I began to settle into my new routine as a member of the team, we would lift weights twice a week, early in the morning, at the South Campus weight room. I quickly realized that being a college athlete was demanding, but it felt like the best job I ever had. Study hall became mandatory for me, and I soon found out how much I needed it. Before being made to go, I hadn't realized how much I was slacking with my study habits. This structured environment was exactly what I needed to get on track.

After every practice, I would stay back to get extra shots in and run through plays, trying to catch up on the playbook.

By Thursday, we were locked in. After practice, as I stayed late with Big Earl, Courtney, and Shannon, Coach Jones called out to me. "Hey, Root! Come here real quick." My heart stopped. I jogged over.

Coach Jones turned to Coach Rike. "Coach Rike, how's Root done this week? Does he deserve to dress out Saturday?"

Coach Rike didn't hesitate. "Yes, sir. He deserves to dress."

Coach Jones looked at me, smiling. "Congrats, son. You're dressing out Saturday. You earned it!"

I was stunned. The dream was real. After all the work, all the waiting, I was going to suit up in a Memphis uniform. I looked up again and silently thanked God. I couldn't wait to tell my family and friends.

First up: my parents. I raced to my dorm, grabbed the landline phone, punched in my calling card number, and dialed home.

"Mom, what are you and Dad doing Saturday?"

She replied, "Probably watching the Memphis game, hoping to see you behind the bench."

I grinned. "How about seeing me in uniform, on the bench, as a Tiger?"

Her scream nearly broke the receiver. "Nathaniel! Are you serious? Are they going to let you dress out?"

I proudly confirmed, "Yes, Mom, I did it! I'm going to officially be a Memphis Tiger!"

THE NEWS

Dad wasn't home from work yet, but Mom promised to tell him the news as soon as he got in. Then came George. "This is just the beginning," he said. "You kicked the door open. Now walk through it."

Next up was Natalie. "Rooty, don't mess with me," she said when I told her. But when she realized I wasn't kidding, her pride came through the line. Even from New Orleans, I could feel her joy.

And then, one more name rose to the top: Bubba. He wasn't just a friend—he was a mentor, a big brother in the game. I dialed. Voicemail. I left a message.

Later that night, the phone rang. Bubba's voice came through, casual at first. "What's up, man?"

"I'm dressing out Saturday."

"You're what?" he yelled. "Now THAT'S what I'm talking about!"

He couldn't make the game—he had one of his own—but his pride rang just as loud. Bubba had been there since the beginning. His belief in me mattered as much as any coach's approval.

That night, sitting on my dorm couch, I felt the full weight of it all. This wasn't just a win for me. It was for everyone who'd believed in me when there was nothing to see. Everyone who'd stayed late, given advice, prayed, or cheered from the stands.

I continued calling all my friends and family, letting them know the good news. Uncle Ned, Grandmother Dean, cousins, friends like Russ, Matt, Rob, Lamont, Doug, everyone I could think of. I finally ran out of minutes on my calling card, but I didn't care. Sharing the news with everyone was worth every penny.

Saturday couldn't come fast enough.

CHAPTER 19

Back to the Beginning

"You spend your life working for a chance, and then it happens. You realize you're living your dream."

Root

February 5, 2000: Memphis vs. Louisville

I had officially checked into my first game as a Memphis Tiger, becoming the first Division I basketball player from my high school. As the announcer called my name, the crowd erupted in a chant that caught me off guard. At first, I thought they were booing, but then I realized they were yelling, "ROOOTTT!"

I stepped onto the court, stunned, the roar of the crowd washing over me. How did they even know who I was? This was my first time dressing out, and yet somehow, the entire arena seemed to be behind me. It reminded me of the movie *Rudy*, that same overwhelming moment when dreams collide with reality and you realize—you belong.

It wasn't just about me. This was Memphis. A city where basketball is stitched into the soul of every street, every neighbor. The fans knew everything. And now, they knew me.

The final buzzer sounded, and the thrill of my debut gave way to the sting of a hard loss. We had fallen short to Louisville. As the energy in the Pyramid faded, so did the illusion that this was my personal moment. I was part of a team now, and my pride in dressing out couldn't overshadow the disappointment of the defeat. The loss hurt, especially knowing how much it meant for Coach Jones, who was fighting not only for wins but for a permanent place as head coach.

We lined up to shake hands with the Louisville team. That's when I saw him—Coach Denny Crum. A legend, a Hall of Fame coach with over 675 wins. As he approached, I felt a jolt of nerves. But when he reached me, he took my hand, leaned in, and said, "Son, I've never seen a crowd do that for a player in person. You need to feel honored."

His words hit hard. Coach Crum had seen it all—and for him to say that about me? That was something I'd never forget. As he let go of my hand and continued down the line, I realized just how significant that moment was. Being recognized by someone of Coach Crum's stature wasn't just an honor; it was a continued validation of all the hard work, the struggles, and the dreams that had led me to that court. The weight of his words settled into my mind, and I knew that this was a memory I would carry with me forever—a moment when a legend acknowledged the beginning of my own journey in a way that only a true master of the game could.

Back in the tunnel, friends and family lined up to slap my hand and shout their excitement. I tried to stay composed—didn't want to come off too eager in front of the coaching staff—but inside, I was lit up with pride.

In the locker room, Coach Jones addressed the team. I braced myself for a harsh breakdown, but he was calm and constructive. He focused on what we could learn, not just what we lost. His approach made it clear why players respected him so much. He wasn't just a coach—he was a steady leader in a storm of emotions.

After showers and a post-game meal, I found my family in the tunnel. The hugs, the high-fives, the disbelief in their eyes—it all meant the world to me. Then, Coach Jones emerged from his media duties. He could've walked right past us. He didn't. Instead, he introduced himself to my mom and dad and thanked them. That gesture, simple but powerful, showed me everything I needed to know about the kind of man he was.

Not far from us, I saw Big Earl with his family. Without needing words, we brought our families together to meet. Earl and I shared more than the court—we shared values, family roots, and now, a journey. His mom, Mrs. Jeraldean, a lifelong educator like mine, and his older sister, Candace, were there with Candace's two children. They embraced my parents like old friends. And with them were his godparents—Snoop and Juanita, or "Gram," who quickly became part of my extended family, too.

That night laid the foundation for a bond between our families that remains strong to this day. It was more than just a meeting of families; it was the beginning of a lifelong connection that would see us through our time at Memphis and beyond.

As we wrapped up the introductions and began walking back through the undercarriage of the Pyramid toward the parking lot, I kept thinking about the surreal events of the night. I wasn't just a practice player anymore. I wasn't just hoping for a chance. I had played—and the crowd knew my name.

On the drive back to campus, Earl riding shotgun in my little lowrider truck, the lights of Memphis lit the sky. I couldn't stop smiling. I was tired, sure—but more than that, I was thankful. Thankful for the opportunity, for the people who believed in me, and for the city that had embraced me so quickly. That night wasn't the end of something—it was the start of everything. The beginning of a new chapter. And I was ready to write it.

CHAPTER 20

Milestones and Moments

"I didn't just wear the jersey—I carried a piece of everyone who helped me get there."
Root

As the season rolled on, my opportunities with the team continued to grow. I was now dressing out for road games—another dream come true. However, this came with a bittersweet reality: Mom and Dad couldn't make those long trips. They didn't have the time or resources to follow the team around the country. Instead, they got a big-screen TV and DirecTV, turning each game into a small hometown event, cheering me on from our living room in McNairy County.

As I scanned through the remaining schedule, two games stood out to me right away: a road trip to New Orleans, where Natalie went to school at Loyola, and another to Tampa, just 40 minutes from George's campus at St. Leo. Both would finally get to see me as a Tiger—something they had both believed in long before anyone else did.

As we arrived in New Orleans, the air felt warm and humid compared to the brisk cold I'd gotten used to back in Memphis. Natalie and I caught up in the hotel lobby after the shootaround. Being together again, even briefly, reminded me why her support always meant so much. That night, Tulane edged us by a single point, and I didn't see the court—but seeing her afterward, her pride still shining, reminded me this journey wasn't just mine. It belonged to all of us. We said our goodbyes, and though it was bittersweet to part ways so quickly, there was something fulfilling about knowing she had been there to witness a piece of this journey.

We snapped our losing streak shortly after with a win versus Charlotte at home, and momentum finally found its way into our locker room. Win after win, our confidence grew. When Tulane came to Memphis for our last home game, we were ready. We crushed them, 77–49. And with three minutes left, a chant began to roll through the Pyramid: "ROOOTTT!" Was I becoming the crowd favorite? Coach Jones grinned and nodded. "Get in the game."

I missed my first shot, but with the next possession, and time running down, I let it fly again—and swish. The crowd erupted. The roar of the crowd was deafening, their cheers echoing off the walls as if I had just hit a game-winner. My teammates mobbed me. It was only one shot in a blowout game, but to me, it meant everything. I was officially in the books. I had scored for the Memphis Tigers.

Afterward, I found my family at the edge of the stands—my parents, grandmother, uncle, and even Earl's mom all wrapped me in hugs and joy. The love in that moment was overwhelming. I was surrounded by people who had believed in me when no one else did.

This was a special group. We weren't just players, coaches, and families—this was a community, a family that celebrated every achievement, no matter how big or small. Tonight, they made me feel as though I was the star of the team, and that meant everything to me. It wasn't just my moment; it was ours.

A week later, we flew to Tampa for our final game against South Florida and Coach Seth Greenburg's tough 1-3-1 defense. George and his crew showed up decked in Memphis blue, cheering before tipoff even began. We executed the game plan perfectly, finishing the first half with a solid 41-35 lead. As the second half wore on, we continued to build momentum, eventually cruising to a commanding 91-72 victory.

With three minutes left, and us up big, I heard them—louder than anyone—"ROOOTTT!" Coach called my name, and I checked in.

MILESTONES AND MOMENTS

As I stood and peeled off my warm-up top, the energy in the crowd seemed to amplify. George and his friends were on their feet, going wild. Chills ran through my body as I stepped onto the court, the roar of my personal cheering section filling my ears. I missed both shots but recorded an assist. It didn't matter. George's pride from the stands was enough to make me feel like I'd just won MVP.

Later, as I made my way out of the tunnel, George, the one who helped me start this dream, who had been there to see it come to life, pulled me aside and said, "This is just the beginning." Those words stuck. For the first time, I didn't just feel like someone chasing a dream—I felt like I belonged. This wasn't just my victory—it was ours. If I never played another minute for Memphis, this night would have been enough.

That night on the flight home, I replayed the game and my brother's words over and over in my mind. The path forward was still uncertain, but I was no longer intimidated by the unknown. For the first time, I didn't just see myself as someone chasing a dream—I saw myself as a Memphis Tiger. And I knew, with unwavering certainty, that more opportunities were coming.

Several days later, we rolled into Conference USA Tournament play with a bit of a spark. The tourney was in Memphis, and our first matchup was a rematch with South Florida—a team we had just beaten. We survived a grind-it-out game and escaped with a 60-58 win.

Earlier in the day, the tournament was rocked by news—Cincinnati's Kenyon Martin, the projected #1 NBA pick, went down with a broken leg. It was a sobering moment, a reminder that this game could be taken from you at any second.

We faced DePaul next, featuring future NBA stars Quentin Richardson and Bobby Simmons, along with a lineup full of future pros. We played with grit, staying within reach, but eventually, they pulled away. We lost 80-76. Just like that, our season was over.

In the locker room, there were tears but also pride. For me, it was a strange mix of gratitude and hunger. I had lived out a dream, but I

ROOT

wasn't done. I had more to give. And after everything I'd learned and experienced, I believed I could be a Tiger not just for one season, but for the next three.

The journey wasn't perfect. But it was real. And it was mine.

CHAPTER 21

The Arrival

"Sometimes the end of one chapter is the beginning of the one you were always meant to write."
Root

The following day, Friday, just before spring break began, the campus buzzed with energy. Students packed their bags, ready to recharge. I was just as eager, looking forward to being back on the farm. But before we could leave, we were called to a mandatory team meeting. Rumors had been swirling about Coach Jones' future, and now, the moment of truth had arrived.

Two possibilities hung heavy in the minds of the players: either Coach Jones would be named the permanent head coach, or the university had decided to bring in someone new. The name we kept hearing was Coach John Calipari.

By the time we were all seated in the conference room, the atmosphere was thick with anticipation. When Coach Jones entered, we could read it on his face before he said a word. His somber demeanor was a stark contrast to the energy he always brought to practice. He began to speak, his voice steady but tinged with emotion. He confirmed what we feared: he wasn't coming back.

The university had chosen Coach John Calipari to take over the program. The room fell into a heavy silence. Coach Jones wasn't just our coach—he was our leader, our motivator, our anchor. He had believed in me when no one else did. Even though I had only played under him for a short time, his impact on me was immeasurable, and my heart broke for him. As we lined up to thank him, I shook his hand and said, "Coach, you made my dream come true. Thank you." His hug in return meant everything.

I drove home in silence, emotions churning. Would Coach Calipari want to keep me on? I didn't know. All I could do was hope.

Midweek, the phone rang. It was Chitra from the basketball office: Coach Calipari wanted to meet with the team Sunday afternoon. I pumped my fist and shouted, "YES!" My parents gave me a puzzled look, but I reassured them: I still had a shot.

The rest of the week flew by. My anticipation grew as I thought about meeting Coach Calipari and what this new chapter would mean for me and the team. Coach Calipari's reputation preceded him. He had led UMass to the Final Four in 1996, then went on to coach the New Jersey Nets. His name carried weight, and I knew he had the knowledge and expertise to develop me into a better player. More than that, if I ever wanted to pursue a career as a college coach, having played under someone like Coach Calipari would be invaluable.

Sunday arrived quickly. The Finch Center buzzed with nerves and excitement. We met part of the new staff—Tony Barbee, Steve Roccaforte, Ray "Rock" Oliver, and Daryn Freedman.

As we made our way into the locker room and settled into our seats, the anticipation reached its peak. Then, the door creaked open, and the room fell silent. Led by his personal assistant, Steve Smith, Coach Calipari entered with a presence that filled the room. There was an undeniable aura of confidence and excitement around him, and you could feel the impact he had on everyone in the room before he even said a word.

With presence and poise, Coach Calipari spoke, "You can call me Coach Cal," he said with a confident smile. His tone was direct. "This first year will be the hardest thing you've ever done. I must make you mentally tough, and some of you won't make it."

He wasn't bluffing. His tone carried no malice, just straightforward truth. He told us one scholarship player had already been let go. That

THE ARRIVAL

hit me hard. As a walk-on, my place was far from guaranteed. This wasn't just a new chapter; it was a completely new book.

Then Coach Barbee announced the first round of early workouts, and my name wasn't on the list. It stung, but I understood. As a walk-on, I knew I wasn't at the top of their priority list, but I also knew this was my opportunity to show my commitment.

Coach Rock then led us to the weight room for a technique session. His energy was intense. His presence was commanding. We drilled fundamentals for an hour. I was locked in, absorbing everything. I left determined to show up the next morning, list or no list.

Walking out of the facility, Earl and Courtney caught up with me. "What are you going to do since your name wasn't on the list?" they asked.

I quickly responded, "I'm going to show up here and be ready to go at 5:00 with everyone else. I'll lift weights with the guards and then work on agility drills during the other hour." I said it with conviction because I meant it.

Earl nodded. "Good plan," he said with a smile.

And Courtney followed up with, "That's what you've gotta do."

When I showed up at 5:00 am with the other two groups, Coach Rock spotted me. "What are you doing here?" he asked.

"I know I wasn't assigned to a group, but I want to be part of this team. I'm here to work and to get better. I am here to prove to you my commitment."

For a split second, his expression was unreadable, but then the faintest grin tugged at the corners of his mouth. "Good," he said simply, nodding his head. That one word was all I needed. It was an acknowledgment, a validation that I had made the right choice.

I joined the guards in their lift, pushing myself harder than I ever had. The weights were heavier than I was used to, and my muscles screamed in protest, but I pushed through. After an hour, I stayed behind to do agility drills. Coach Rock noticed. He said he might need help with the post group next. I was exhausted but fulfilled. I was proving I belonged.

Coach Cal added another layer to our routine: team breakfast. It wasn't just about food; it was about unity. That morning, he laid out the classroom expectations: be on time, sit in the front row, don't leave early, and participate. If one guy slipped, we all paid. Later that day, someone did.

We were back in the gym at 5:30 am the next day for "20-20s"—20 suicides in 20 minutes. Coach Cal continued explaining, "We'll put twenty minutes on the clock. When I say go, you have 35seconds to complete a suicide. Then, when the clock hits 19:00, you go again. We keep going until the clock hits zero."

I had never pushed my body that hard. By the end, we collapsed. The message was clear: accountability mattered.

Study hall was mandatory too. Five nights a week, no excuses. While others grumbled, I embraced it. My GPA climbed from the edge to a 3.5 by year's end. I was proud of that.

The rhythm set in: early lifts, individual skill work, breakfast, classes, study hall, followed by afternoon pickup games. It was relentless but transformative. I grew more confident. I was earning my place.

The next Monday, I showed up early again with the rest of the team even though I was not in a group. I was in the weight room when Coach Roccaforte called out, "Let's go, Root. Coach Cal wants you on the floor."

I froze, then hustled out thinking to myself, "Why would Coach Cal want the shortest player on the team out there with the big men?" The post group was short a man, and they needed me to keep the groups even and give the other three guys a natural break during reps. I dove into screens, seals, post moves—everything. It pushed me, but I loved it. At the end, Coach Cal said, "Keep showing up. If we need a spot filled, you're in."

That small recognition fueled me. Every rep mattered. This was a game-changer for me. Learning the nuances of their position gave me a deeper understanding of the game. It forced me to see basketball from a new perspective and challenged me in ways I hadn't expected.

Week by week, I improved. The team improved. Coach Cal

didn't just teach plays—he taught the game. Footwork, angles, reads, discipline. I began to see basketball on a whole new level.

For me, this experience was unlike anything I had ever been part of before. In high school, basketball practices had been centered around team drills—learning plays, running scrimmages, and preparing for the next opponent. However, the focus here was on developing each player individually. It was about developing skills that not only strengthened the team but also helped us grow as basketball players.

The camaraderie among teammates deepened, too. We held each other accountable, lifted each other up, and shared in every success. We were more than a team. We were becoming a unit.

By the end of the semester, I wasn't just a better basketball player—I was a better version of myself. I had grown in ways I hadn't expected, both on and off the court. The discipline, the work ethic, and the determination I was developing weren't just preparing me for the upcoming season—they were preparing me for life.

CHAPTER 22

From the Finch Center to the Pyramid

"The grind never stops, and neither do the ones who want it bad enough."

ROOT

The summer of 2000 wasn't a break—it was the beginning of a grind. Coach Cal required every player to enroll in at least two summer classes. His reasoning was simple: we were already on campus lifting, running, and playing pick-up games—so why not get ahead academically before the travel-heavy season hit?

But basketball and books weren't the only focus. Coach Cal had arranged internships for us at FedEx—not in the warehouse, but in corporate offices, where we observed meetings and studied logistics. It was a crash course in professionalism, a reminder that we were more than athletes. We needed to prepare for life after basketball, and this gave us a rare head start.

Coach Cal's staff continued to grow, too. Derek Kellogg, one of his former players at UMass, joined as an assistant. Then came Milt Wagner, a Louisville legend and NBA champion. His presence added weight to every workout—we were learning from someone who had been exactly where we hoped to go.

Our days were tightly packed. Workouts started at 7:00 or 8:00 am, depending on class schedules. After weights or skill sessions, we grabbed breakfast and hustled to class. By 11:00 am, it was time for pick-up games at the Finch Center. Then from 1:30 to

5:30 pm, we were at FedEx. It was nonstop. Grueling. But it was also molding us.

During June, youth basketball camps brought hundreds of kids into our orbit. After their sack lunches, they'd pack the gym to watch us play pick-up. What had been loose summer runs transformed into heated battles. Kids cheered every dunk, every deep three-pointer and crossover, and even a few boosters started sneaking in. The atmosphere lit a fire under us. Every day became a tryout—another chance to prove we belonged.

I was still technically a walk-on. I hadn't been told outright that I was on the team for the coming season. But I was there every day—lifting, running, interning, playing. I figured that meant something.

By July, the energy in our pick-up games started to fade. We needed new competition. I reached out to old friends—Bubba, Matt, Gaylon, and Steve, plus a few others who were still playing college ball or had recently graduated. We set up a run at Union University in Jackson first, and then they came to Memphis for the second trip. It was exactly what we needed. The matchups were fierce, both sides trying to prove who had the edge.

After trading home-and-home runs between Union and Memphis, the bond between our groups grew. It reminded me how basketball had always connected us. Even outside the program, we found ways to push each other and get better.

As August approached, we got a short break to go home. I soaked up time with my family and recharged. But even in that quiet environment, I stayed focused. I got shots up, played pickup with hometown guys, and mentally prepped for the firestorm I knew fall would bring.

When I returned to campus, the air buzzed with new-year excitement. Coach Cal had upgraded our living situation—out of the dorms and into on-campus apartments. Each unit had four bedrooms, two bathrooms, a kitchen, and a common area. It felt like a big leap forward.

Most of the team got placed together. I, however, was still a walk-on, so I was assigned to an apartment with some of the team managers.

FROM THE FINCH CENTER TO THE PYRAMID

They were great, but I wanted to live with Earl and Courtney. Still, I didn't complain. I was close to them, and that was enough.

That evening was the back-to-school block party—a Memphis tradition. Thousands of students filled the streets, music pulsed, and the energy was wild. After I got settled in my room, I changed quickly and made my way over to Earl and Courtney's apartment. They were rooming with two seniors, Shannon Forman and Shyrone Chatman, both of whom were from Baton Rouge, like Courtney. We all sat around for a bit, talking about the upcoming season, our new living arrangements, and, of course, what the night had in store.

As the sun dipped below the horizon, we started making our way toward the block party. As we approached the entrance, where campus police had blocked off the streets, people started recognizing us. Students rushed over, shaking our hands, giving us hugs, and even pulling out their disposable cameras—this was before iPhones and social media were a thing—to snap pictures with us. Every few minutes, someone would yell out, "Go Tigers Go!" The love from the student body was overwhelming. In that moment, we felt like celebrities.

Eventually, we ducked into the Sigma Phi Epsilon house, where I was a member. It was quieter there, a good place to hang out with friends without the chaos. Later, one of the brothers snuck us out the back door so we could get home without wading through the crowd again. Welcome week was officially over, and now the real work began.

With the excitement of the back-to-school weekend behind us, reality quickly set in. Preseason conditioning was going to be a beast. Cal hadn't been exaggerating when he said this would be the hardest thing we've ever done. The dreaded 20/20s returned—each run a predetermined number of seconds to complete suicides. Coach Rock crushed us in the weight room. Individual drills focused on every weakness. Nothing was wasted. Every step, every rep had purpose.

As fall deepened, two words pulsed in our minds: Memphis Madness.

This annual event marked the start of official practice, and Coach Cal had a new plan. Instead of a single night of hype, we'd have to earn it—two full practices on Saturday, another one on Sunday morning, and then Memphis Madness Sunday night.

This year's guest? None other than Dick Vitale.

The Pyramid buzzed as we arrived. We were led into a private room filled with boosters and Rebounders Club members, all of whom were shouting and clapping as we entered. It felt like something big was happening—because it was. Memphis basketball wasn't just back—it was becoming a movement.

When Dick Vitale walked in, the energy jumped even higher. His larger-than-life personality took over the atmosphere. He shook hands, cracked jokes, and reminded us of the stage we were on. We took pictures, laughed, and soaked it all in. Then it was time to change into our gear and get ready for the big show.

Inside the tunnel, the arena went black. Spotlights danced. Smoke hissed. "Eye of the Tiger" blasted through the speakers. Flames burst from the backboards. This wasn't practice—this was theater.

Then came Chuck Roberts' voice, unmistakable and electric. His signature introductions had been a staple of Tiger basketball, and tonight, he was in peak form. One by one, he introduced the team.

I started to become nervous. Would the home crowd remember me from the end of last season? I wasn't a highly touted recruit or a returning starter. I was still just a walk-on. Would they cheer for me the way they did for the others?

As my name appeared on the jumbotron—"NATHANIEL ROOT"—the arena roared. For a moment, it sounded like they were booing. But no. It was "ROOOTTT!"

The chant rolled through the Pyramid like thunder. It hit me hard—these fans remembered. These fans cared.

As I sprinted out to join my team, smiling widely, I realized something had shifted. I wasn't just part of the team anymore.

I was part of Memphis.

I had become their fan favorite.

CHAPTER 23

Earning My Stripes

"When your time comes, you have to be ready."
Kobe Bryant

After the electric energy of Memphis Madness and the first grueling weekend of two-a-days, it was time to dig in. Coach Cal had warned us: the next two weeks would test us mentally and physically. Practices stretched over three hours during the week, with two-a-days on weekends. These weren't just workouts—they were battles.

This level of intensity was new to me. We weren't just running plays or getting in shape—we were studying NBA-level strategies. Every session was layered with detail: defensive rotations, offensive reads, and new terminology. I had no margin for error. A scholarship player might get a pass for a missed assignment—I couldn't.

After weeks of relentless training, we finally got a taste of live competition. Our first exhibition game was against the Universal All-Stars, a team of former college players, including former Memphis Tiger Jermaine Ousley. The crowd gave him a standing ovation—proof of how deep Tiger pride ran.

We led by 9 at halftime, but the All-Stars clawed back early in the second half. During a timeout, Coach Cal unleashed one of his signature fire-up speeches, and we responded with a 10-0 run—Earl igniting the charge. With the game winding down and the win secure, I heard the crowd again. The deep, thunderous sound rising from the Memphis faithful.

ROOT

"ROOOTTT!"

Coach Cal looked my way and nodded.

I checked in with just a minute left. The crowd erupted. I got one clean look—a three. It didn't fall, but the fans loved it. I belonged out there. The game ended 77-61, and while the scoreboard showed a win, our real reward was the film room and another chance to sharpen our play before the next exhibition.

We got back to work over the next several days, focusing on correcting the mistakes we had made in our first exhibition game. Coach Cal emphasized attention to detail, making sure every cut was sharp, every defensive rotation was crisp, and every possession was executed with purpose. We knew we had one more tune-up before the regular season, and we wanted to be as prepared as possible.

Against Team Georgia, we tightened things up and played with greater discipline. With that win, we turned our attention to the real season opener: a nationally televised home game against Temple, coached by the legendary John Chaney. The history between Chaney and Coach Cal ran deep—and sometimes heated—but this game was about mutual respect and the start of a new chapter.

The Pyramid was rocking—over 20,000 fans, ESPN cameras, and the energy of a city ready to rise. This wasn't just a season opener; it was a statement game for our program. We jumped out strong, leading by 9 at halftime, but Temple's zone defense picked us apart in the second half. They went on a 14-2 run, and though we fought back, we fell short, 67-62.

It stung, but we had no time to dwell. In six days, we'd be in Puerto Rico for a tournament stacked with top-25 teams. We opened with a scrappy win against Miami University of Ohio, but then ran into a juggernaut—#5 Stanford. The Collins twins, future NBA players, dominated the paint, and Casey Jacobsen torched us from the line. They beat us soundly.

Next came #13 Utah. We came out hot, built a 12-point lead, but couldn't hold it. Another second-half collapse ended in a narrow 61-58 loss. We left San Juan 1-3—disappointed but clear-eyed about what needed fixing.

EARNING MY STRIPES

I didn't get the opportunity to step onto the court, but the experience of traveling to a place I had never been, competing in a high-stakes tournament, and bonding with my teammates made all the hard work leading up to this moment worth every minute. I knew my time would come—I just had to keep grinding.

Back home, we barely survived a flat first half against UT Martin before exploding for a 28-5 run to put it away. Late in the game, I heard it again: "ROOOTTT!" I checked in, but I didn't get a shot up. Still, a win was a win, and we needed it.

Then came a brutal stretch—three games in eight days against #25 Arkansas, #6 Tennessee, and our rival, Ole Miss. We battled hard but lost the first two. Before the Ole Miss game, we learned that three of our key players would be out for an extended period. The news hit hard—losing them would challenge our depth in a big way. Coach Cal pulled me aside the day before: "Root, I'm going to need you tomorrow. Be ready." I nodded, heart pounding.

The next night, midway through the first half, he called my name. I checked in, ran the offense, applied pressure, and stuck to the plan. Several minutes later, when he subbed me out, Coach Cal said, "Great job. Be ready—I'm putting you back in to finish the half."

Late in the half, I got the ball with the clock ticking down. My passing option was covered. Instinct took over. I drove baseline and let the jumper fly.

Swish.

The buzzer sounded. The Pyramid erupted. I jogged off the court, my adrenaline pumping, into a storm of high-fives from my teammates and coaches.

We came up short in the end—64-56—but that moment felt like a breakthrough. Coach Cal trusted me. I wasn't just a body in practice. I was part of the rotation.

My minutes went up against Arkansas State. I played 10 minutes, scored 1 point, and helped settle the offense. We won big—83-60—and followed it with another dominant showing against Christian Brothers. That night, I got hot: 3 threes, 9 points—my career high.

With every bucket, the "ROOOTTT!" chants grew louder, fueling my confidence with every possession.

Walking off the court that night, I felt a sense of growth. I wasn't just a walk-on filling minutes anymore—I was contributing. With back-to-back wins, our team was starting to find its rhythm.

We carried that momentum into a road game against Miami. The Hurricanes were a talented squad led by future NBA players James Jones and John Salmons. We opened on a 10-0 run but couldn't sustain it. Miami adjusted, took the lead by halftime, and pulled away with a 25-7 burst in the second half. Another tough road loss, but the focus shifted quickly—Conference USA play was beginning.

Our opener against Southern Miss was another gut punch. Down to eight available players, we scrapped to stay close but couldn't close the gap late, losing 75-67. Sitting at 4-8 overall, 0-1 in conference, this wasn't how we wanted to end the year (2000). But we weren't giving up.

Twice-a-day practices over Christmas break pushed us to the brink. But we kept grinding, knowing our moment was coming. The results weren't there yet, but deep down, we knew it was only a matter of time before we broke through. We just had to keep believing, keep working, and trust that our moment was coming.

CHAPTER 24

The Streak

"You may encounter many defeats, but you must not be defeated. In fact, it may be necessary to encounter the defeats, so you can know who you are, what you can rise from, and how you can still come out of it."
MAYA ANGELOU

Just three days after a tough loss, we faced Kansas State at home—our final game of the year. Determined to close out the year on a high note, we poured everything into extra practices. That work paid off. We led by 7 at the half, then caught fire in the second, scoring 53 points and cruising to an 81-58 win.

Coach Cal didn't wait for the crowd to chant "ROOOTTT!" this time. With just over five minutes left, he called my name. The arena erupted. I knocked down a deep three and added a free throw, soaking in the roar of the fans. It felt like we'd finally turned a corner.

We opened 2001 with a non-conference game against Howard, and we didn't let up. By halftime, we led by 27. When senior Marcus Moody scored our 101st point with minutes to play, the place went wild. We had done it—our first time breaking the century mark since 1994. We closed the night with a 112-42 win—our largest margin in years. I logged 14 minutes, scored 3, and handed out 6 assists. Even more special: I helped set a new school record with our 15th made three-pointer.

Conference play resumed on the road against Houston. Earl stepped up with a career-high of 24 points, leading us to an 86-78 win, our third in a row. We were now 7-8 overall and finally gaining momentum. A gritty win over DePaul in Chicago, led by senior guard Shyrone Chatman, brought us to .500. They still had future NBA talent on their roster, but this time, we were ready. Back home, we added two more nail-biters—one in OT against Saint Louis and another tight one against Houston.

Now 10-8 overall and 4-1 in conference, we were riding a six-game streak. Our cohesion, forged through early adversity and Coach Cal's relentless preparation, along with our extra hours in the gym, was finally paying off. Next, we headed to Tulane, where my sister, Natalie, was in the stands again. Late in the game, I buried a three-pointer—my only shot—and could hear her and her friends cheering, their energy making it feel like a home game. After the win, I managed to sneak in a quick hug and visit with Natalie and her friends before we headed straight back to Memphis.

But there was no time to celebrate. The next day, we flew to Birmingham to face UAB. The Bartow family history with Memphis gave this game extra weight. Coach Bartow's father, Gene Bartow, had once led Memphis, so there was always extra intensity in these matchups. We trailed most of the way but forced overtime, then gutted out a win to extend our winning streak to eight.

Back in Memphis, 12-8 overall and 6-1 in the conference, we felt unstoppable. The struggles of the early season felt like a distant memory. We were now facing Marquette in a battle for first place. The Pyramid was booming with nearly 18,000 fans. We fought, but Marquette edged us out, 71-65, ending our run. The loss stung—especially at home—but we had to bounce back. Coach Cal reminded us that great teams don't let one loss turn into two.

Next up: South Florida in Tampa. My brother, George, was in the crowd again, which gave me all the motivation I needed. We broke the 100-point mark again, winning 100-89. I didn't score, but playing in front of George was enough. I kept writing "III" on my shoes—my quiet tribute to him, and he noticed. He gave me a quick hug before we had to leave. He whispered in my ear, "Thanks! That means a lot."

THE STREAK

We returned home to face Tulane again, and this time, we dominated from the start, winning 91-64. I played nine minutes and scored two baskets. Coach Cal didn't wait for chants—he subbed me in on his own. That didn't stop the fans from erupting in cheers when I checked in. It was a small sign that I had earned my role and the minutes I was receiving.

That win pushed us to 14-9 and 8-2 in the league. But next up was our biggest test: Cincinnati. ESPN primetime. National stage. 19,000 fans in the Pyramid. Cincinnati was led by the legendary Hall of Fame coach Bob Huggins and featured a ferocious backcourt, Kenny Satterfield and Steve Logan, both future NBA draft picks.

It was a battle from start to finish. With 15 seconds left, we led by one. But Kenny Satterfield hit a falling, off-balance jumper with 0.9 seconds left to steal the win. We'd fought with everything we had—and still came up short. Just like that, Cincy had snatched victory from us once again, dealing us a crushing blow and knocking us out of first place in the conference.

A tough road loss to Charlotte followed, and suddenly, our place atop the standings was in jeopardy. With only four games left, we needed wins to secure a top seed in the tournament.

Against UAB at home, we came out flat. It was our third game in five days, and exhaustion was setting in, but there were no excuses. Coach Cal lit into us early, and we responded. I checked in late to the usual "ROOOTTT!" chants but missed a three. Still, we won comfortably. Then we took care of South Florida, improving to 16-11 and 10-4 in the conference.

But the regular season ended on a low note. We dropped back-to-back road games to Southern Miss and Louisville—Coach Denny Crum's final home game, no less. The crowd in Freedom Hall was on another level, and we couldn't overcome it.

Despite the losses, we locked up the No. 4 seed in the Conference USA Tournament, earning a first-round bye. Our opening game was a rematch with Marquette, who had beaten us earlier. This time, we jumped out early and held on late, winning 71-64. In the locker room,

Coach Cal didn't celebrate. "One game at a time," he reminded us. "Your only goal is to win and advance—nothing else matters."

Next came Cincinnati. The revenge game. From the jump, it was a slugfest. But their backcourt of Satterfield and Logan was relentless, combining for 56 points. We threw everything at them, but they answered every run. Final buzzer: another loss. Our conference run was over.

Sitting in the locker room afterward, all I could think was: Was that it? Without the tournament title, an NCAA bid was unlikely. We had fought so hard. Were we done? Would we get one more chance to put on the Memphis jersey, especially for the seniors who had given their all to this program?

But a few days later, our season was given new life: an NIT invite.

And just like that, the season continued.

CHAPTER 25

No Excuses

"The only limit to our realization of tomorrow is our doubts of today."
　　　　　Franklin D. Roosevelt

We got the call that Sunday, and we were heading to Salt Lake City to face Utah in the NIT. It wasn't March Madness, but it was a second chance, especially for our seniors. We were locked in, ready to extend our season.

But then, during our last practice, just before departure, I came down wrong on a teammate's foot during a rebound drill. A sharp pop. Instant pain. My ankle swelled fast—a high ankle sprain. Ray, our trainer, rushed me to the training room, submerging my ankle in a bucket of ice to stop the swelling. But the damage had been done. My ankle had ballooned to the size of a softball. Still, I flew with the team, ankle still swollen, doing everything I could to heal.

In Utah, I taped it tight and limped through shootaround. I wasn't sure I could go, but I suited up anyway. I hadn't missed a game due to injury since my junior year of high school, and I wasn't about to start now. Thankfully, my teammates handled business. We beat Utah 71-62. I didn't play—but I was ready if they'd called my name.

Back in Memphis, Coach Cal gave us the next few days off—a much-needed break for everyone. The break became a rehab marathon for me—ice, compression, stretching, and therapy with Ray four times a day. Ray told me to skip the next practice. But when Coach Rock saw me in the training room, his quiet disappointment hit harder than any yell: "I never thought I'd see the day where you wouldn't practice."

That was all it took. The guilt hit me instantly. My body told me I needed another day. Our trainer had told me I needed another day. But I couldn't shake Coach Rock's words. I couldn't let him down.

"Tape me up," I said to Ray.

I got taped up and practiced, pain and all. It hurt badly, but I pushed through every drill. Afterward, Coach Rock told me, "I knew you could make it through. That's why I said what I did. You just set an example for the rest of this team—no excuses, no shortcuts." That meant everything to hear those words come from him.

When UTEP came to town for a second-round match-up, with only 14,000 fans in attendance, the Pyramid was rocking. We dominated start to finish, winning 90-65. I was able to log six minutes of action, and when I got my chance, I let a three-pointer fly—and buried it. The fans erupted, their cheers echoing through the arena. No matter how many times it happened, hearing that reaction never got old. It was more than a basket—it was Memphis showing me love.

Two nights later, we played for a trip to Madison Square Garden. With five guys in double figures, we crushed it—81-63. Kelly and Earl dominated the paint in our last home game. The crowd roared "ROOOTTT!" one last time with under three minutes left in the game.

Among the crowd that night were a few people from my hometown who had made the trip to watch me play. As they cheered, they struck up a conversation with some fans sitting nearby. As I stood at the scorer's table, waiting to check in, one of the fans turned to the group and said, "This Root kid can flat-out shoot the basketball. Just watch what he does in these last two minutes."

The group, laughing, responded, "Who, Root? We know him. The coach wouldn't let him shoot in high school."

Seconds later, I caught the ball deep beyond the arc, squared up, and let it fly—nothing but net. The Pyramid erupted. The same fan turned back to the group and said, "Maybe he should've been shooting. Because he can definitely light it up at this level."

NO EXCUSES

Next stop—Madison Square Garden. The Mecca. Growing up in rural West Tennessee, I never dreamed I'd play there. MSG, home to the New York Knicks, the stage where every basketball great had left their mark, was now going to be my stage, if only for a brief moment. Michael Jordan, Larry Bird, Magic Johnson, and Allen Iverson had all dazzled under these same bright lights.

Allen Iverson, one of the most electrifying and culturally influential players of our time, had a direct connection to us. Through his endorsement deal with Reebok, we were the only Iverson-sponsored team in the country. From our jerseys to our shoes to our travel suits—everything we wore carried the AI brand. Walking into the Garden, decked out in Iverson gear, added another surreal layer to this moment. We weren't just playing in MSG; we were representing one of the biggest names in basketball.

In the semis, we faced Tulsa and fell behind by 20. We stormed back to within 3 points but couldn't finish the comeback. A 72-64 loss—but not the end. The NIT offered a consolation game for third place.

We'd face Detroit. Rashad Phillips led them, but we were locked in. We shut down everyone else, holding them scoreless for over seven minutes. With minutes left, we were up 69-53, and it was clear: we were going out winners. I had never ended a season with a win before, and as a team, we all felt a responsibility to send our seniors—Shannon Forman, Marcus Moody, Shyrone Chatman, and Shamel Jones—out the right way.

Then came my moment. The "ROOOTTT!" chants echoed—not just from Memphis fans, but others in the arena too. Coach Cal looked down the bench, locked eyes with me, and gave me his usual nod. I checked in. I missed two threes but hit both free throws. I had scored in The Garden.

The final buzzer sounded. We had won. Our seniors got their moment. I got mine. And we all walked off that court, knowing we'd left something behind in Madison Square Garden.

CHAPTER 26

Earned, Not Given

"You don't get what you wish for. You get what you work for."
Root

After the season ended, something shifted in me. I wasn't just a walk-on anymore—I was a legitimate Division I basketball player. I had logged career highs in minutes and points, been called on in meaningful moments, and somehow become a fan favorite. The Pyramid would erupt with chants of "ROOOTTT!" whenever I checked in—a sound that never stopped surprising me.

All I had wanted at the start of the year was a few garbage-time minutes. Maybe a shot or two. But I had earned far more than that. I had earned my place.

Coach Cal gave us a few weeks off before the grind picked back up, but even during that break, the energy around the program was building. We were bringing in a top recruiting class—McDonald's All-American Dajuan Wagner, freshmen Anthony Rice and Duane Erwin, JUCO star Chris Massie, and Antonio Burks, who had sat out the previous year. Memphis was suddenly on every preseason radar, projected as a Top 12 team.

As summer began, Coach Cal hosted a team cookout at his house across from our apartments. After dinner, he gave a few updates, then paused. "One more thing," he said. "I'm putting Root on a full scholarship."

My jaw dropped. My teammates erupted, cheering, hugging me,

and patting my back. I was stunned. I had earned it. I was officially a Division I scholarship athlete.

As if that moment couldn't get any more surreal, I found out I'd also be switching jersey numbers—from 4 to 32. It was the same number I had worn with pride all throughout high school, a number that carried deep meaning for me. It reminded me of where I came from, the roots I never wanted to forget, and all the people who had helped me along the way. Wearing 32 again felt like coming full circle—and I couldn't have been prouder to be putting it back on.

Summer workouts intensified. The city buzzed with basketball—between the Grizzlies' arrival and our daily pickup wars in the Finch Center, Memphis was alive. Morning lifts, conditioning, classes, then midday pickup games that felt more like playoff battles. Trash talk flew, egos clashed, and reps were earned.

Lorenzen Wright, "Ren" to us, was a fixture in those games. His passion and toughness were contagious. In one heated game, he drew a double team and kicked it out to me. I hit the shot. Next play—same thing. Another three. Then I heard him shout, "Y'all better not leave my white boy! Make 'em pay, Root!" That moment rewired something in me. If an NBA vet trusted me to hit big shots, then I needed to start trusting myself more.

From that point forward, I trained like a shooter. Reps, footwork, release—I wanted to be automatic. If I was going to contribute next season, it was going to be as a shooter. I had to be automatic. By late July, I wasn't the same kid who had shown up just hoping to survive. I wasn't the biggest, the strongest, or the most athletic player on the team, but I had one job—stretch the floor, be ready, and knock down shots when my number was called.

The summer closed with something special; Memphis hosted the first-ever Penny Hardaway Basketball Camp. Penny and Coach Cal partnered up to unite the city's basketball legacy with its future. Despite the extra activity, our routine stayed the same. Morning workouts. Class. Mid-day pickup games.

My mom came to visit that week and to watch us play. She was a former Memphis athlete herself, so she understood the grind. As I walked into the court area, I scanned the bleachers for her to see where she was sitting. I heard a voice: "Hey Root!" The voice was unfamiliar. I turned—and it was Penny Hardaway.

He walked over and shook my hand like we were old friends. I stammered, "How do you know who I am?" He smiled and said, "Man, I keep up with you guys. I've known who you were since your first game." I was shocked. This was a player I had grown up watching, a player whose jerseys I had collected, a player I had idolized—and he knew who I was. It didn't seem real.

Later, I looked over during our scrimmage and saw Penny sitting next to my mom, chatting like old friends. When I asked her what they talked about, she said they had a 20-minute conversation about Memphis sports, family, and life. That moment stayed with me. Penny didn't just acknowledge me—he acknowledged my mom. It wasn't just about basketball—it was about being genuine, professional, and connected to the Memphis community. That single interaction left a lasting impression on me, reinforcing the idea that true greatness isn't just measured by talent, but by the character behind it.

As the week ended and I packed for a two-week break, I was blessed to meet someone who would become a lifelong friend—Nafeesa Farrakhan. From Chicago, she was coming to Memphis in the fall to not only go to school but also to help with the day-to-day operations in the basketball office. Her encouragement, loyalty, and friendship meant more than she probably even knows, and I'll always be grateful she was part of my journey. I carried all of that with me: the new friendship, workouts, the confidence, the scholarship, and the moment with a childhood idol who had become a mentor without even knowing it.

Returning for the fall semester, I felt good. Confident. Ready. Then, a gut punch—Courtney Trask, one of my closest friends on the team, called me to his room. His eyes told me everything before he even spoke. "Root, I'm transferring," he said quietly.

I was stunned. We had been through it all together. Practices. Bus rides. Locker room talks. He was there for me from the beginning, continuously pushing me. He explained it was about fit, about doing what was best for his future, and that he was going back home to Baton Rouge to play for LSU.

We hugged it out, trying to fight the emotion. Later that night, Earl and I sat in silence, both of us feeling the weight of losing part of our foundation. But we understood. Basketball is family, but sometimes family members follow different paths. We swore to be family for life. No matter where basketball took us, we promised to always have each other's backs. And to this day, we are still family.

We plunged into preseason. And as always, Coach Cal didn't ease us in. From the first day, it was grueling—suicides, lifts, full-speed drills. Your legs ached. Your lungs burned. There were days when our legs felt like cement blocks and every muscle in our body ached, leaving us to wonder if we could actually make it through another session. But somehow, we always did.

Coach Cal had this way of saying things that stuck. "Don't just get through the workout to get through it. Get better," he'd bark. Or, "Don't dread the grind—learn to love it." At first, those words felt like coach-talk. How were we supposed to "enjoy" something that left us gasping for air and struggling to walk to study hall afterward? But over time, we got it. It wasn't just about the body. It was about the mind and breaking through mental barriers. Push through the fatigue, and you'd find out who you really were.

He pushed all the right buttons. He demanded more from us than we thought we had. But we gave it—because we knew he believed in us.

Then came Memphis Madness.

This year, we weren't in the Pyramid. We took it back to where it all began—the historic Mid-South Coliseum. It was about honoring the legacy: the 1957 NIT Finalists, the 1973 NCAA Finals team, the 1985 Final Four squad, and the 1992 Elite Eight team. We weren't just introducing our team—we were connecting to history.

EARNED, NOT GIVEN

Walking into that Coliseum, shoulder-to-shoulder with some of the greatest players to ever wear the Memphis jersey, was surreal. These were the men I watched growing up while sitting on the floor of our farmhouse, glued to the TV. These were faces I had seen on old posters, names I had memorized from years past.

Now, I was one of them.

We hadn't played a single game yet, but we could feel it—this season was going to be different. It wasn't just about potential. It was about purpose. We weren't just building a team. We were continuing a legacy.

CHAPTER 27

Falling Short, Aiming High

"The expectation of others can be heavy, but the expectation you put on yourself is even heavier."
Root

The early grind of the season was no joke—three-and-a-half-hour practices during the week, two-a-days on weekends. We were pushed to the limits, but we were locked in, hungry for real competition. Exhibition play brought our first test, and we crushed Team Georgia and the Universal All-Stars with ease. Our chemistry, depth, and intensity were evident. This team was different—we were dangerous.

Opening the regular season at home, we rolled through Wofford, Old Dominion, and Northwestern State. Kelly Wise, Earl, and Chris Massie dominated the paint. Dajuan Wagner, our prized freshman, dropped 32 against Old Dominion, showing why he was the most hyped recruit in the country. Fans were fired up. So was I. The chants of "ROOOTTT!" still came each night, but something wasn't right.

My shots weren't falling.

In each game, I had a chance, but the ball wouldn't go down. In the first game, I went 0-1 from three. In the second, I managed just 1-2 from the free-throw line. In the third, another 0-1 from beyond the arc. I had spent all summer working on my shot, getting up hundreds of reps every day. The gun-shooting machine had practically become my best friend. I was knocking them down in practice, but when it came to the games, they just weren't falling.

I could feel the weight of expectation—from the crowd, from my teammates, from the coaching staff, and from myself. I didn't want to let them down. But deep down, I knew I had to stay the course. Shooters shoot. I just had to keep working, keep trusting, and the shots would start falling.

Next stop: Kansas City for the Coaches vs. Cancer Classic. Our first game was against #9 Iowa, a gritty squad led by future NBA big man Reggie Evans and Luke Recker. We battled, matching their physicality, but their experience edged us out in the final moments—75-72. A tough loss, but no time to sulk.

The next night, we faced #22 Alabama. They had five players score in double figures, led by future NBA All-Star guard Mo Williams and Rod Grizzard, a future second-round NBA draft pick. They moved the ball well, and despite our fight, they pulled away late, 81-70. Two straight losses. Just like that, we dropped from the national rankings. Expectations were sky-high, and we were underperforming.

As we boarded the private plane back to Memphis, there was a quiet determination in the air. The early-season setbacks had only fueled our fire. We had three upcoming games at home—three chances to right the ship, regain our momentum, and show everyone that this Memphis squad wasn't going to fade away. We needed a reset.

Southeastern Louisiana was first, and while we were sloppy, we got the win. Christian Brothers was next—my chance for redemption. I'd had a breakout game against them the year before. I was ready. Coach subbed me in with five minutes left. Five minutes was plenty of time for me to get a few shots up, or at least I thought. I moved without the ball, found open looks, and stayed patient. I got one three off—it felt good—but rimmed out. No make. No roar from the crowd. I walked off frustrated.

I thought to myself, if only the Memphis fans knew how much I wanted it, how much I wanted to give them that moment. I was happy for our wins, but I couldn't shake the disappointment in myself. I had spent countless hours in the gym, getting up shots before and after practice, yet the results weren't coming when it mattered most.

FALLING SHORT, AIMING HIGH

The final game of our three-game home stretch was against Eastern Kentucky. We steamrolled them, putting up 111 points. I played six minutes but didn't even get a shot up. I tried not to let it shake me. I kept working. Kept grinding.

Our next challenge was Ole Miss in Oxford—a close, physical game. Every possession felt like a war. We came up just short, 71-67. Another missed opportunity.

Eight days later, we were back in the Pyramid for a showdown with Tennessee. Over 18,000 fans packed the arena. We controlled the game most of the way, building an 11-point lead late. But Tennessee surged back, closing the gap quickly. We held on—barely—winning 71-69. The crowd went wild, knowing we were sending the Volunteers back to Rocky Top with an L. The energy in the building was raucous, and we weren't ready to let it go.

That night, we hit Beale Street.

We'd been before, but this time was different. As we passed Blue City Café, the "Go Tigers Go!" chants grew louder. Fans stopped us, asking for pictures and autographs. It didn't matter that I hadn't played. They treated me like a star. The love was real. That night, I felt what it meant to be embraced by a city.

Sunday brought a day off, but I couldn't rest. I needed reps. I needed to find my rhythm. Earl joined me at The Finch Center, and we hit the gun for a shooting challenge. First to 10 makes. He was a 7-footer with a three-point stroke, and he was on fire. So was I. We pushed each other, shot after shot, game after game. It was the most fun I'd had all week. And if you ask who won, I am going to say I remember beating him, and I'm sure he would say he remembers beating me.

That Monday, the team was buzzing. Confidence was back. In the locker room before practice, Coach Cal gathered us. This time, it wasn't about X's and O's—it was about how the world perceives winners versus losers.

"When you win, and you win at a high level, everyone looks great," he started. "Everyone is a star. Even Root—he doesn't get the minutes you all do, but in this city, he's a rockstar. I can't go anywhere without someone asking me why I don't play him more."

We all laughed.

"But when you lose?" he paused, "Suddenly, none of you can play. Suddenly, I can't coach. That feeling you had Saturday night? You want to keep that? Then keep winning."

He was right. Winning changes everything. It silences critics. It energizes the city. And it gives each of us our moment to shine. I was still waiting on mine, but I knew it was coming.

CHAPTER 28

Big Moments, Bigger Lessons

"Success is no accident. It is hard work, perseverance, learning, studying, sacrifice, and most of all, love of what you are doing."
Pelé

Our mid-season trip to Philadelphia for a matchup against Temple wasn't just another road game. It was a homecoming for Dajuan Wagner and Arthur "OG" Barclay, both Camden, New Jersey legends who had led Camden High to the 2000 South Jersey Group 3 championship. We all felt the importance of that moment and wanted to show out for them.

The day before the Temple game, Coach Cal, having spent time on the Philadelphia 76ers staff under his coaching mentor, Larry Brown, before coming to Memphis, took us to a 76ers practice. Watching Allen Iverson up close changed how I viewed greatness. He was my size but played like a giant—every drill, every possession, he went full speed. It wasn't just talent; it was his intensity, his heart. It was inspiring to witness firsthand.

After their session, we took the floor. Practicing on an NBA court energized us. I kept thinking about Iverson's fire. If one of the league's best players still practiced like that, what excuse did I have not to go all-in?

We handled Temple with toughness, grinding out a 64-54 win behind our defense. It was especially meaningful for Dajuan and OG, who got to celebrate in front of their hometown fans. But the night got even more surreal back in the locker room.

ROOT

Waiting for us was William "Uncle Wes" Wesley, and with him, Jay-Z. Coach Cal didn't recognize him at first and nearly kicked him out before Uncle Wes clarified things. Jay-Z greeted every player, offering encouragement like we were his own. First Iverson, now Jay-Z? My basketball journey had officially entered dream territory.

Back home just two days later, we faced Austin Peay. Fueled by those Philly moments and watching Iverson work, I hit the gym hard. I knew my shot was coming.

Midway through the second half, Coach Cal put me in. The crowd of 18,000 fans didn't even have to start their customary "ROOOTTT!" chant—I was already at the scorer's table. And when I buried my first three of the season, the Pyramid erupted. Then I hit two more. Three threes and four assists later, I left the floor to a standing ovation.

We only dressed 11 guys that year, which made our bond tight. Everyone had each other's backs. The way our starters celebrated my buckets showed just how connected we were.

Our final game of 2001 was against UT Martin, and this time, we dominated from start to finish. With just under two minutes left, the now-expected "ROOOTTT!" chants were rolling through the Pyramid. I checked in with under two minutes left. As I walked past Coach Cal, he looked at me with a smirk and said, "Let it fly." I knew exactly what that meant.

As I walked onto the court, a UT Martin sub leaned over and said, "The crowd won't be cheering for you tonight. I'm not gonna let you get a shot off."

I didn't say a word—just nodded and smirked. But in my mind, I thought, he obviously doesn't know me too well.

First possession: catch, shoot, swish.

Second: same thing.

Third attempt? Fouled while shooting, making two of three free throws.

8 points in under two minutes. The arena was shaking. In back-to-back games, I had given the Memphis faithful what they wanted. But

something shifted in me. I wasn't just riding a high—I was feeding off the hype, and it was going to my head.

After the game, I signed some autographs and took some pictures with fans and then linked up with two of my best friends, Matt and Bubba, who had attended the game. I was carrying myself differently, feeling untouchable, like a superstar.

Bubba pulled me aside and said, "Root, don't let this go to your head. Don't forget where you came from. Don't let this attention change who you are."

His words hit me like a punch to the gut. He was right. I was letting the success, the crowd's adoration, and my recent performances inflate my ego. I needed a reality check, and my best friend was the one to provide it. A true friend will always be honest with you, even when it's not what you want to hear. And over the years, I've thanked him more times than I can count for keeping me grounded when I needed it most.

We rang in 2002 with a tough loss to Arkansas. A physical, foul-heavy game unraveled on us late. We lost our edge and took a 90-73 defeat. It didn't feel like us, and it was clear we needed a reset.

We were still 4-1 in our last five games, and deep down, I think we all knew what needed to be done. So, just like the year before, we got back in the gym. Extra shots before and after practice. Time in the weight room. We knew we couldn't afford to coast. Not now.

Our first conference game was against Southern Miss, who had beaten us twice the year before. This time, we made sure it wasn't close—75-53. 1-0 in conference play.

Next up: TCU in Fort Worth. Instead of the usual hotel meal, we were welcomed into the home of Coach Barbee's aunt, Jennifer Matthews—Aunt Jenny, as we called her. That night was full of warmth and laughter with her family. That feeling followed us to the court. We gutted out a 98-93 win and improved to 12-4 overall and 2-0 in conference play.

Our chemistry was building. We were 6-1 over our last seven games and rolling into New Orleans to play Tulane. But for me, it meant seeing my sister again. She was there with friends, holding up signs in the stands as usual. That never got old.

As we got ready to take the court, I opened the locker room door and nearly ran into someone. Standing right in front of our locker room was a familiar face. I had seen this guy before, but for a second, I couldn't place where.

He dapped me up and said, "What's up, Root. Go handle business."

I was stunned. It was Lil Wayne, the New Orleans rap superstar.

He knew who I was. He knew everyone on the team.

We won the game 78-70, but all I could talk about afterward was Lil Wayne. My sister laughed when I told her and her friends about meeting him—another memory for the books.

We kept winning—two more victories pushed us to 15-4 and 5-0 in the conference. The extra workouts, the shooting sessions before and after practice, the relentless commitment to improving—it was all paying off. Then came UAB at home.

Coach Cal called us in before practice. Antonio Burks and Dajuan Wagner had been late to class, and he wasn't starting them.

He turned to Ant Rice, a freshman and one of my roommates. "You're starting."

Then to me. "Root, you're starting, too."

I could barely believe it. My first Division I start.

I had spent my entire career being the guy who came in late in games when we were up big. I had gotten reserve minutes here and there, but now I was about to take the floor as a starter for the Memphis Tigers in front of nearly 18,000 fans.

I called Dad: "Hey, Dad, don't tell Mom, but I'm starting tomorrow. Don't tell her. Just come so it will be a surprise."

He brought a surprise for me as well—James Dennie, a family friend from back home. Mom still had no clue. Later, Dad told me that just minutes before the game started, my mom had looked up at the jumbotron and noticed something strange.

She turned to my dad and asked, "Why do they have Nathaniel's number 32 up there for the starting lineup?" Dad, trying to keep a straight face, shrugged. "I don't know."

Then, the moment arrived. The first chords of "Eye of the Tiger" blasted through the arena speakers. The energy in the Pyramid was electric.

One by one, my teammates were announced.

Then, I heard it:

"Starting at guard, a six-foot junior, from Adamsville, Tennessee, number 32, Nathaniel… ROOOTTT!!"

The entire Pyramid erupted in cheers, filling the arena with their deep, rumbling "ROOOTTT!" chant.

Dad said Mom started screaming and grabbing him by the arm. "George, he's starting! Did you know this?"

Dad had to come clean.

As I stood in the spotlight during introductions, I expected nerves to hit me, but surprisingly, they didn't. I was calm. Focused. Ready. I reminded myself of one simple truth—every day in practice, I went up against two of the best guards in the country. If I could compete against them every day, I was ready for anything.

The ball soared into the air as Kelly Wise tipped it my way. I caught it cleanly and settled into my role, setting up the offense like I had done countless times in practice. We executed our first play, feeding Kelly in the post, but his shot rimmed out.

UAB tried to establish their rhythm, but our defense was locked in. A tough contested shot clanked off the rim, and as the ball bounced out of bounds off UAB, I instinctively glanced toward the scorer's table. I fully expected to see a sub waiting to check in for me—this was, after all, my first start, and I figured my minutes would be short-lived. But there was no one there. Instead, I saw Coach Cal on the sideline, shouting out instructions and motioning for me to stay focused.

As I approached half court, I could hear the chatter from UAB's defense. They were scrambling, adjusting their matchups. Their game plan had been built around guarding Antonio Burks, but with him not in the lineup, they had to make quick decisions.

"Double off of 32! Double off of 32!" I heard them yell.

ROOT

I almost smirked. They had no idea what my role was on this team.

We reran the same play, getting Kelly the ball on the left block. Just like their coaches instructed, my defender abandoned me, sprinting down to help double-team Kelly. I instinctively slid up to the top of the key, ready. Kelly, being the high-IQ player he was, saw the trap coming and fired a crisp pass my way.

Without hesitation, I caught it, squared up, and let it fly.

Swish.

The Pyramid erupted. The sound hit me like a tidal wave, the kind of roar you dream about as a kid shooting in the driveway. My teammates on the bench jumped up, clapping and cheering, and as I jogged back on defense, I locked eyes with Dajuan Wagner and Antonio Burks—two guys who were supposed to be starting but were now my biggest supporters.

We had jumped out to a 12-5 lead. The first 7 points had come from Anthony Rice and me, the two players no one expected to start that night. Coach Cal let me run with the starters for the first five minutes before finally calling for a sub. As I came off the court, I was met with a wave of high-fives, pats on the back, and words of encouragement.

By the end of the game, we had dominated UAB, 102-81. I ended up with two threes and a win in my first start. More than that, I saw my family and friends beaming from the stands. I locked eyes with one of my closest friends—Tamika "Red" Rogers—as she came running over to the side of the tunnel. She leaned over with that signature energy only she had. She wrapped me in a big hug and said, "I'm so proud of you, Root." In that moment, it wasn't just about basketball—it was about the years of friendship, support, and belief she'd shown me. Red was more than a friend—she was like a sister, and having her in my corner made that night even more special. I had come from a small town with no recruiting buzz, walked onto my dream school, fought for every opportunity, earned a scholarship, and now, I had started a game at the Pyramid. My journey up until now was proof that with enough heart and dedication, you can turn dreams into reality.

I wasn't supposed to be here. But here I was. And I wasn't done yet.

CHAPTER 29

Bringing It Home

"Basketball, like life, doesn't let you coast. You either adapt, or you get left behind."
Root

With our season hitting stride, we were 16-4 overall, undefeated in conference play at 6-0, and had won 10 of our last 11 games. The chemistry we built over time was showing, and confidence was high.

We rolled into Houston and handled business with an 84-66 win—seven straight wins. But the big one was next—Louisville at home. That rivalry always brought out the best in us, and we rose to the moment, grinding out an 80-70 win in front of a fired-up Pyramid crowd.

TCU and Tulane came to town next. Against TCU, we dominated wire-to-wire, winning 98-72. I even knocked down a three-pointer late, and the crowd erupted. Then came Tulane. As we warmed up, I spotted Lil Wayne sitting courtside. I made sure to connect with him this time.

As he was dapping me up, I said, "Good to see you again," still slightly in disbelief. Then I asked him straight up, "What brings you to our game?" He grinned and said, "Man, I love coming to Memphis. Y'all got a squad. I've been keeping up with y'all all season." I told him we appreciated his support and that he was always welcome to come whenever he wanted.

We also won that game, 78-72, extending our win streak to nine.

Then came the road trip that derailed everything. UAB came out swinging and handed us a humbling 64-46 loss. A few days later, Charlotte beat us too, 75-63. Returning home, we hoped to bounce back against Houston but fell short again, 76-73. From nine straight wins to three straight losses—it was a gut punch. Now, with only three games left before the conference tournament, we were spiraling. Something had to change—immediately.

We finally got back on track with a 71-59 win at South Florida. Then came senior night against DePaul, Kelly Wise's last home game. We played inspired and ran them off the floor, 88-61. I only played a minute but hit one of two threes, wanting to contribute however I could.

Our last regular season game was a shot at redemption—a road game at #4 Cincinnati. A win could boost our NCAA tournament hopes. It was a battle. The game was everything ESPN could have hoped for—an instant classic. Both teams traded blows from start to finish, neither willing to back down. Burks hit two clutch free throws to give us a 68-66 lead with 6.9 seconds left. One stop away from a massive win. But Steve Logan hit a tough shot to force overtime, and we couldn't recover, losing 80-75.

We weren't guaranteed an NCAA tournament spot anymore. In the conference tournament, we had earned the No. 3 seed, received a bye, and were scheduled to play Houston. From the opening tip, Houston controlled the game. Every time we made a run, they answered. They never let us take the lead, staying one step ahead with their defensive intensity and timely shot-making.

We fought until the end, but Houston sealed the game at the free-throw line, knocking down every crucial attempt late in the game. The final buzzer sounded, and we walked off the court stunned.

Houston beat us 72-67. Now, all we could do was wait.

Selection Sunday at Coach Cal's house was tense. One by one, the bracket filled. Our name was never called.

Silence.

BRINGING IT HOME

Then Coach Cal got a call.

"We're in the NIT," he told us. "If you want to prove the selection committee wrong, go win the whole thing."

And just like that, our new mission began.

We opened against UNC Greensboro in the Pyramid. Fueled by frustration, we took them down, 82-62. Next up: BYU. They were tougher, but we pulled away late, 80-69. One more win, and we'd be heading to Madison Square Garden for the second straight year.

Tennessee Tech came in ready to upset us. They weren't intimidated by our crowd, and defensively, we weren't at our best. But when it mattered most, we dug deep and made the right plays. We held on and won 79-73. We were New York-bound.

Our semifinal at the Garden was against Temple. From the opening tip, it was clear this was going to be a battle. This one went down to the wire, but we edged them—78-77—thanks to Dajuan Wagner's 32-point performance. He carried us.

That set up the title game against a tough, physical South Carolina team. Earl was unstoppable in the first half—9-for-9 shooting and 19 points. I was going crazy on the sidelines, cheering louder than anyone. Not only was he my teammate, but he was one of my closest friends. Seeing him dominate on the biggest stage, in the biggest game of our season, was special. We led by 6 at the break and never gave it up. We closed out a 72-62 win, capturing the first national postseason title in school history.

As time was winding down, Coach Cal gave me the nod. I checked in for the final moments and got to be on the court when the buzzer sounded. I had played in Madison Square Garden two years in a row, and now I was part of a championship team. As we celebrated on the court, cutting down the nets and holding that championship trophy high, I knew this win was more than just a team win. This was for our program, our history, and more importantly, this was for the city of Memphis.

Back in Memphis, the airport was packed, overflowing with fans. The energy in the building was explosive—people were cheering, waving signs, and wearing their Memphis blue with pride. It was the kind of homecoming you dream about, a moment that felt bigger than just basketball. Before we got off the plane, the coaches asked, "Who's carrying the trophy?" The whole team shouted, "Let Root carry it!" I was caught off guard, but my heart swelled with pride. My teammates, my brothers, wanted me to be the one to carry our hard-earned championship back home.

I walked off the plane with that trophy in my hands, walked through the security checkpoint, and was greeted by thousands of fans. High-fives, hugs, photos—it was surreal. We had brought a championship back to Memphis, and the city celebrated.

This wasn't just our title. It belonged to the city.

It belonged to Memphis.

CHAPTER 30

Resilience Over Regret

"The moment you're ready to quit is usually the moment right before you succeed. Don't ever give up."
ROOT

We spent the spring celebrating our NIT championship, soaking in every bit of it. Memphis embraced us with open arms—parades, fan events, and recognition at Redbirds games. One of the first people to come and see us when we returned to campus was John "J White" White. A longtime friend and Tiger through and through, J White had always been in our corner. Fun-loving, energetic, and the life of the party, he told us in his unforgettable voice, "Fellas, I'm proud of you! But remember, y'all ain't nothing—but y'all all we got!" I still laugh when I think about it.

But even as we basked in the victory, reality hit hard. Dajuan Wagner, our star freshman, declared for the NBA draft. We also lost two incoming stars—Amar'e Stoudemire and Qyntel Woods—who opted to go straight to the league. In a single offseason, we lost three future NBA players. Dajuan went sixth, Amar'e ninth, and Qyntel twenty-first. We were happy for them, but there was no denying the impact this would make. Our Final Four dreams for the next season took a massive blow.

Coach Cal and his staff wasted no time. He rebuilt with a new class led by Memphis native Jeremy Hunt, along with Rodney Carney and Almamy Thiero. John Grice and Billy Richmond became eligible after sitting out the year before. We still had a squad, but the city's excitement began to wane. I felt that the city's expectations lowered, but inside our locker room, belief stayed strong. We were Memphis. We were built on grit.

The summer became a turning point. Our daily pickup games were battles—intense, balanced, and always down to the wire. Antonio Burks and I picked teams every day, and it brought out the best in everyone. We bonded in the grind, both on the court and at our FedEx internships. Then came a moment none of us saw coming.

One afternoon in June, the coaches called us in for a surprise evening session. No explanation—just be there and be ready to play. Earl and I were both working at the same FedEx building, and I tracked him down immediately. "You know what's going on?" I asked.

"No clue," he replied.

That evening, I was already in the gym, ankles taped, shoes laced up, ready to go by the time Burks came strolling in. As he sat down to put on his sneakers, his back to the gym doors, I caught sight of a tall figure entering. It only took a second for me to recognize who it was.

I glanced down at Burks and smirked. "I got Magic. Your pick."

Burks furrowed his brow. "What?" he asked, turning around.

The moment he saw who I was talking about, his eyes widened. NBA Hall of Famer Magic Johnson had just walked into our gym, shoes in hand, ready to play.

He was in town early for the Tyson-Lewis fight at the Pyramid and called Coach Cal to see if we wanted to hoop. So, there we were, running a pickup with an NBA legend. Magic took over instantly, running the floor, dishing no-look passes, and hitting guys in perfect rhythm. I didn't even think I was open half the time, yet the ball hit me in the shooting pocket every time. It was like he saw the future. For one night, I was teammates with Magic Johnson—and we didn't lose a game.

The experience reminded all of us why we grinded the way we did. Magic made it look effortless, but his greatness was in the details, in the decisions, in how he elevated everyone around him.

RESILIENCE OVER REGRET

Starting the fall semester of my senior year, we were no strangers to the grueling preseason workouts, the relentless conditioning, and the mental challenges that came with being part of a Coach Cal-led program. Grizzlies guard Jason "White Chocolate" Williams joined us for a conditioning session. We had been running 20/20s for weeks—sprints that drained every ounce of energy. Jason, having spent his summer just playing pickup, outlasted all of us. He never slowed down. He never bent over. He just kept going. His motor was relentless. Watching him made something click with our team: talent alone wasn't enough. Greatness required a higher motor from everyone.

The season was fast approaching, but before we could even get started, more adversity hit. Several key players were ruled out for the first few games. They were able to play in the exhibition matchup, but after that, they had to sit. That meant more minutes would need to be spread around. I figured Coach Cal would give me an extended run in the exhibition games to get ready.

But that didn't happen.

For the first time in my career, I didn't play a single minute in an exhibition. It crushed me. I had always earned time in those games. I had worked my tail off that offseason, and now, I was left sitting on the bench, waiting to hear my name, but it never got called.

That night, something I had never felt before crept in—I wanted to quit.

I should have talked to Earl, Big Red, or Ant Rice about it. They were my roommates and my closest friends on the team, but I didn't want to vent to them. The next day, we arrived at the Finch Center for practice, only to find out that Coach Cal had canceled our afternoon session and rescheduled it for 5:30 the next morning. That gave me time to think, and I knew I couldn't keep this to myself anymore. I had to talk to Coach.

When we sat down in a side room, I told him, through tears, "Coach, I don't know if I want to do this anymore," I admitted. "I've never had this feeling before, but after not getting in the game last night, it just hit me."

His response was sharp but real.

"Root, if you quit, you'll regret it the rest of your life. Everything I do, I do for a reason. Don't let last night define your role. You've got until morning. If you're not at practice, I'll know your answer."

Those words hit hard.

That night, I sat in the living room with my roommates. We didn't talk about the game or Coach's decision. We talked about life. Big Red reminded me of who I was, what I'd earned, and how far I had come. They didn't sugarcoat it, but they didn't let me spiral either. They believed in me, and that mattered more than anything.

Even now, as I think back to that moment, I am disappointed that I ever allowed myself to become that mentally weak. That wasn't me. That wasn't how I had been coached in high school, and it wasn't the mindset that had gotten me to Memphis in the first place.

More than anything, I thought about my brother. He would have traded places with me in a heartbeat. He would have died for this opportunity, and here I was, on the verge of walking away. This wasn't just about me. This was about my teammates, who were my brothers on and off the court. This was about the commitment I had made, the sacrifice it took to get here.

The next morning, I was the first one in the gym.

When Coach Cal arrived, I walked up and told him, "I'm sorry. I'm good to go."

He just nodded and patted me on the shoulder. That was all I needed.

That practice wasn't any different in terms of intensity, but for me, it was everything. I had stared down a moment of weakness and chosen to rise instead. The road ahead was still uncertain, but I wasn't backing down. I was still here. Still fighting. Still believing.

That's what Memphis basketball and the whole city were about.

CHAPTER 31

Moments That Define Us

"I've missed more than 9,000 shots in my career. I've lost almost 300 games. Twenty-six times I've been trusted to take the game-winning shot and missed. I've failed over and over and over again in my life. And that is why I succeed."
MICHAEL JORDAN

We returned to Madison Square Garden for the third straight year. This time, it was to open the season, but somehow it felt different. We had made a pact as a team: this would be our last trip to the Garden unless it were for the NCAA Tournament. No more NIT. No more settling. We were ready to prove we belonged.

Our opponent was Syracuse, stacked with talent—Carmelo Anthony, Gerry McNamara, and a battle-tested roster. To make things harder, we were missing two or three starters. Still, we had hungry freshmen like Jeremy Hunt and Rodney Carney ready to step in.

Coach Cal had a plan. During practice leading up to the game, he pulled me aside and said he was going to use me in a unique role offensively. I would slide in at the power forward spot to help stretch the zone and shift our senior John Grice to the wing. He believed Grice's shooting would force Syracuse out of their traditional 2-3 zone and open the floor. But to everyone's surprise, Syracuse opened in man-to-man.

Then, Rodney Carney made a statement—posterizing their seven-footer on our third possession. The place erupted. Syracuse quickly switched to their signature 2-3 zone, putting Cal's plan back in motion. Moments later, with Anthony Rice in foul trouble, Coach Cal called my name.

Before the game, legendary announcer Dick Vitale saw my platinum blonde hair and asked if he could call me "Eminem" on air. I laughed, a little star-struck, and told him, "You can call me whatever you want." I had bleached my hair platinum blonde, looking like Eminem in his prime. Sure enough, the moment I checked in, "That's Eminem, baby!" boomed across the broadcast.

At the first media timeout, we were up 11-5 and clicking. From there, we exploded. Jeremy Hunt was slashing through the paint, Grice was knocking down NBA-range threes, and suddenly, we were up 30-13 halfway through the first half. We were chest-bumping, high-fiving, playing loose and fearless. We didn't just believe we could hang with Syracuse—we believed we could beat them.

I played nearly the entire first half, held my own defensively, and helped move the ball. I didn't score, but I was part of a group that built a big lead. Then Melo turned it on, scoring 15 straight to cut our lead. At the half, we were up 9 points.

I didn't play in the second half, but we held strong. Syracuse made a run, but we responded with a 12-0 spurt to seal a 70-63 win—a total team effort. We scrapped, we fought, and we wanted it more. We didn't have our full roster, and it didn't matter. We were 1-0 to start the season. A powerful start. Coach Cal came into the locker room after the game and reminded us, "You can't go undefeated if you don't win the first one."

But the celebration was short-lived. Jeremy Hunt broke his foot, and other players remained out. Coach Cal gathered us at practice and went over the game plan for our next matchup: Austin Peay. Then he looked at me and said, "Root, you're starting."

My second career start wasn't ceremonial. We were down to seven players, and I had to deliver. Austin Peay was coming in looking for the upset. As tipoff approached and we lined up for introductions, I heard my name boom across the PA system. This time, there was no surprise. The Pyramid filled with that familiar chant—"ROOOTTT!"

The game stayed close. We went into overtime tied, and with 3.9 seconds left, we had the ball and a chance to win. The play was for Earl, who had a career-high 26 points and had been unstoppable, but something broke down. The ball came to me.

I pulled up from deep. Missed.

It wasn't how I wanted it to go. I felt like I had let everyone down—my teammates, my coaches, the fans, and the city. But walking through the tunnel, I reminded myself: even MJ missed game winners. I went to bed already planning the comeback.

Over the next three days, I spent my time in the gym. Before practice. After. Late nights. Just me, the ball, and the goal. I wasn't just chasing my shot. I was chasing my confidence.

On game day, Mark Goodfellow—a diehard Memphis sports fan—pulled me aside. "Forget the last game. Keep shooting. You've got this." I smiled, nodded, and thanked him. I had already put the loss behind me, but something about his words gave me an extra lift, like the city still believed in me. That belief meant more than anyone knew.

That night, I didn't start, but I played 26 minutes. I shot 4-7, including 3-5 from three. 11 points. My first time hitting double digits.

We won big, 78-54. Help was on the way, but I had done my job.

As our roster stabilized, we started to gel. We handled Arkansas-Little Rock and Furman easily. Then came #11 Missouri. We weren't ready. They jumped on us 15-0 and never looked back. Final: 93-78.

Next came Ole Miss at home. With over 18,000 fans behind us, we gutted out a gritty 58-51 win.

Then came the week we had been waiting for. Senior power forward Chris Massie and Jeremy Hunt returned just in time to face #7 Illinois. This wasn't just any top-10 team—we were facing a team led by Hall of Fame coach Bill Self, with a starting five that all went on to play in the NBA. Their star point guard, Deron Williams, would go on to be a three-time NBA All-Star. The Pyramid was packed with over 19,000 fans in attendance. But we weren't intimidated. We were Memphis. A blue-collar team ready to fight for every possession. Ready to battle.

We trailed at half but stormed back. We won 77-74. The Pyramid erupted.

Students stormed the court, surrounding us in a sea of blue and white. We huddled at midcourt, jumping, hugging, celebrating—not just the win, but everything that led up to it. The injuries, the early losses, the questions—this moment silenced all of that.

We were 6-2 and whole again.

Fresh off the emotional high of beating #7 Illinois, we knew we couldn't afford to let our guard down. Our next matchup came just two days later—a home game against Murray State. Tied at half, concern in the building. Massie took over—15 points, 10 boards in the second half. We survived, 67-60.

Then Fayetteville. A road war with Arkansas inside the electric Bud Walton Arena. We stayed composed, played tough, and pulled out a 72-67 win.

Next was Villanova and their star Randy Foye. They couldn't contain Massie, and we beat them 72-68. That made five straight. We were 9-2. Every win was building our identity—tough, together, and unshaken.

Conference play began against Tulane. Our offense was sharp, and we cruised to an 85-73 win—six in a row.

Then came the stumble.

At Southern Miss, we led at halftime but collapsed, giving up 55 points in the second half. Final: 84-67. Still shaken, we lost a one-point heartbreaker to South Florida at home, 75-74.

We bounced back against Houston with a solid win, 77-66, but the inconsistency lingered. On the road at Saint Louis, we dropped another tight one, 69-66.

Now 11-5 and 2-3 in conference, we were at a crossroads.

We needed to rediscover our identity. Tough. Gritty. Together. There was still time, but we had to fight like our season depended on it.

Because it did.

CHAPTER 32

The Final Chapter

"You'll never forget the final moments."
Root

With a rare whole week between games, we reset—physically and mentally. Coach Cal pushed us hard, drilling us on the details: defensive rotations, communication, and shot selection. He reminded us that it's often the small things, not the big ones, that win or lose games. Stay focused.

When Southern Miss came to town, we made sure they didn't embarrass us again. We jumped out to a 13-0 lead and never looked back, winning 80-62 with a statement. That energy carried over as we rolled through East Carolina, TCU, and Tulane—five straight wins, including a tight one in New Orleans that marked the last time my sister saw me play in a Memphis uniform. It meant more than I could say.

Back home against UAB, we were locked in, crushing them 94-70. We were 16-5, 7-3 in conference, and jelling. Then came our biggest test: a road trip to #4 Louisville, led by Hall of Fame Coach Rick Pitino. We hit the glass hard, out-rebounded them 47-31, and gutted out an 80-73 win. That one felt special. NCAA-level special.

We still weren't shooting free throws well, and it nearly caught up to us at South Florida. But we escaped with a 73-66 win and followed it with a blowout over TCU. With a minute left, I heard it again—"ROOOTTT!" Coach Cal nodded. I checked in. One possession, one shot, one make. The place erupted. And just like that, I realized it was almost over. My time in a Memphis jersey was almost up.

One home game left.

We were 19-5, 10-3 in the league, on an eight-game win streak, and #24 in the nation. Cincinnati was coming. This one was for first place in the division. Every possession was going to matter. Coach Cal, true to form, told all four seniors we'd start. I looked at Earl, my roommate and my best friend. We were going to share the court one last time. That Saturday felt like it moved in slow motion. I didn't want the day to end. I wasn't ready to say goodbye to the fans who had cheered my name with so much passion, the same way they had for our top players.

The Pyramid was packed. National TV, ESPN, the works. As we burst out of the tunnel and stepped onto the floor, I looked up and saw a sea of blue—every single seat filled. Almost 21,000 fans in attendance. The lights, the energy, the chants. The crowd was electric. Then the familiar chords of "Eye of the Tiger" roared through the arena.

When the announcer called my name, the crowd exploded, and the building shook. "ROOOTTT!" It hit me like a flood—four years of sweat, sacrifice, and moments like this.

I played the first few minutes, then checked out. As I was walking off the court for the final time in the Pyramid, I could hear the crowd rise and cheer. Not just politely. Genuinely. Loudly. With love. That moment... I'll carry that forever. We dominated 67-48. Afterward, the four seniors huddled at half court, arms wrapped tight. Earl said it best: "It's been a fun ride... but we've still got work to do."

And we did.

We closed out the regular season with road wins at Houston and UAB—11 straight victories, 22-5 overall, 13-3 in conference. We were the 2-seed for the Conference USA Tournament and ranked #18 in the country.

In Louisville, for the conference tournament, we opened with a gritty 62-56 win over South Florida. That set up a semifinal showdown

THE FINAL CHAPTER

with Louisville. It was a war. It was a back-and-forth slugfest. Bodies on the floor. Lead changes. Momentum swings. It was the kind of game that defined March. With 32 seconds left, we led 74-71. But in a painful blur, they stole it—78-75. The locker room afterward was silent. The dream of a conference title was gone. All we could do was wait.

On Selection Sunday, we gathered at Coach Cal's house, nerves high. When "Memphis" popped up as a 7-seed playing Arizona State, the room erupted. Finally, we were back in the NCAA Tournament—for the first time since 1996, when Tiger legends Chris Garner, Cedric Henderson, and Lorenzen Wright were playing.

Arizona State had a monster in Ike Diogu. The first half was a slugfest—15 lead changes, tied at 33. It was playing out like a true 7-10 matchup. But in the second, Diogu dominated. They opened on a 13-2 run, and we couldn't recover. We cut it to five, but they always had an answer.

And then, with a few minutes left, it hit me.

This was the end.

Coach Cal looked at me and gave me the nod. I checked in for the last time. I soaked it all in—the lights, the hardwood beneath my feet, the crowd. I wasn't just ending a game. I was closing a chapter I'd written that started with just a dream.

After the final buzzer, we shook hands and walked off. Coach Cal thanked us and told us he was proud of us. But I could hardly hear him. I was overwhelmed. This was it. My emotions poured out. Tears I couldn't hold back. The kind that come when you give everything you have to something, and now it's over.

Earl, Massie, and Grice would have opportunities to play professionally. Overseas contracts, maybe even the NBA. But for me? I didn't. Though it hurt, I was thankful.

I was an unrecruited player from small-town USA. A walk-on turned scholarship player. A fan favorite. A champion. A Tiger through and through.

As I pulled off my jersey for the last time, Earl turned to me, locked eyes, and said, "We walked in together for your first game as a freshman. We're walking out together for our last."

And we did—shoulder to shoulder, two Tigers, two best friends, one last walk, and a lifetime of memories.

The End

EPILOGUE

"Always let your ambitions further, never overshadow, your accomplishments."

Root

I hope everyone has enjoyed my story. Writing this book has been a deeply personal journey—one that began not on paper, but in a dream that started more than 35 years ago on a farm in McNairy County. I was just a kid with a ball and a vision: to wear the Memphis Tigers jersey. That dream came true. And now, so has another one.

For the past 15 years, it's been on my heart to write an inspirational book—something that could speak life into others the way so many moments and people have spoken into mine. It wasn't just about basketball. It was about faith, perseverance, friendship, and the quiet strength of trusting God's timing, even when we don't understand it.

There were seasons I thought I knew exactly what I wanted. I chased certain goals with all I had—only to learn that sometimes, what we want isn't what God wants for us. And that's okay. Because what He has planned is always greater. Always better. It just takes time—and trust—to see it.

So, if you're holding onto a dream, chase it with everything you've got. Pour your heart, your soul, and your effort into it. But if it doesn't unfold the way you imagined, don't be discouraged. That detour might just be God's direction. He sees the bigger picture. And He's never late. He's never early. He's always right on time.

This story was mine—but maybe, just maybe, you've found some of yours in it too.

Life After the Dream

After my playing days at Memphis came to an end, I found myself lost. Like so many former athletes, I was met with the unsettling question: What now? The only dream I had ever chased—playing basketball for the University of Memphis—was over. I had lived it. I had felt the roar of the crowd, worn the jersey, and walked off the court for the last time. But now that it was done, I didn't know what came next.

I needed a new purpose. New goals. A new dream to chase.

Deep down, I knew I wanted to stay close to the game that had shaped my life. I didn't care in what capacity—I just knew I wanted to be part of the basketball world. So, I took my first step into coaching, accepting the head coaching position at Memphis Catholic High School. It wasn't glamorous. It wasn't big time. But it was basketball. It was mentorship. And it was a new beginning.

Not long after, my phone rang. On the other end was Tony Barbee, one of my former assistant coaches at Memphis. He had just taken the head coaching job at the University of Texas at El Paso (UTEP), and he asked me to join his staff. I didn't hesitate. I packed my bags, got in my car, and made the 15-hour drive west.

What followed were four of the most rewarding years of my life. Together with Coach Barbee, Tony Madlock—who I had grown up watching play at Memphis—Randall Dickey, Mike Babul, and Milt Wagner (Dajuan's father and a former assistant under Coach Cal), we built a championship program at UTEP. In the 2009-2010 season, we won the Conference USA regular season title and earned a spot in the NCAA Tournament. But it wasn't just the wins. What truly made those years special were the relationships—with the staff, with our players, and with the people of El Paso.

I'll never forget the warmth and generosity of the El Paso community. The city's rich Hispanic culture and close-knit spirit made me feel right at home. People like John Matsko, Paul Petersen, Danny and Laura Sander, Mike and Sue Mendoza, Amanda De La Torre, and Mike Mendoza welcomed me like family. I didn't just coach basketball

EPILOGUE

there—I lived, grew, and built lifelong friendships. To this day, those relationships remain some of the most meaningful in my life.

After our success at UTEP, Coach Barbee accepted the head coaching job at Auburn—and once again, he brought me with him. It was another incredible opportunity, but after just one year, I made the difficult decision to leave. That staff was more than a team; they were family. Walking away from that group of men was one of the hardest decisions I've ever had to make.

Since stepping away from Division I coaching, I've continued to pour into the game in other ways—coaching at different levels and providing skill development training to young players chasing dreams of their own. Along the way, I also stepped into a new world—working with Bob Smith at Quail Systems, helping introduce industry-leading ozone cleaning and disinfection technology. It was different from basketball, but it stretched me in new ways, and I was grateful for the experience.

Then, in the fall of 2021, life came full circle. I joined forces with my twin sister, Natalie, as a consultant at her company, The Root Agency. Working alongside her has been one of the greatest joys of my professional life. I've learned so much from her—about leadership, strategy, and innovation in the nonprofit space. Her unique 4-D approach to fundraising—Development, Data, Design, and Delivery—is changing the game. Together, we've helped our clients raise over $100 million, empowering organizations to fulfill their missions and transform communities.

While continuing to work with my sister at The Root Agency, I've also found a way to stay connected to the game that built me—through private, individual basketball lessons. Getting back in the gym, teaching all aspects of the game, and mental preparation has reignited something in me. It reminded me of why I fell in love with the game in the first place—not just for what it gave me, but for how it allowed me to pour into others.

I owe a special thank you to Reese Gladish for getting me back into basketball training. Reese's belief in me—and her dad, Bart Gladish's, willingness to push me back toward the game—helped me rediscover the excitement I didn't even realize I was missing. That spark led to something deeper than just drills and gym sessions—it brought purpose back into my relationship with the game.

I'm also incredibly thankful to Maddie Kirk and Lena Taylor. Working with them individually, helping guide their development, watching their confidence grow—it's been a gift. Through every workout, every conversation, and every breakthrough, they've reminded me that mentorship is one of the most powerful forms of coaching. These three players—Reese, Maddie, and Lena—have trusted me with their development, but the truth is, what they've given me in return can't be measured. They've restored my passion for the game, and for that, I'll always be grateful.

In addition to basketball and consulting, I've also stepped into a completely new arena. I've started a home furnishing business in McNairy County called Home Solutions Warehouse. It's a new chapter. Through this venture, I've been able to provide quality kitchen cabinets and home essentials that help families turn their houses into homes. It's not just about products—it's about providing solutions with integrity, affordability, and care.

These last several chapters of my life have taught me that dreams don't end—they evolve. I didn't know it then, but when I walked off the court for the last time in that Memphis jersey, I wasn't closing the book. I was simply turning the page.

New Friendship

One of the unexpected blessings of life after Memphis basketball has been the people I've met along the way—none more meaningful than my close friend Rhamen Love-Lane. We met after my playing days, but it feels like we've known each other our whole lives. He didn't just become a friend—he became part of our extended family. The kind of person you don't just hang out with, but lean on. The kind who shows up when it matters most.

Rhamen's story is impressive in its own right. A standout dual-sport

EPILOGUE

athlete at Wake Forest, he played both football and basketball at the Division I level—something very few can claim. But beyond his talent, it's his humor and loyalty that have always stood out. He's the type of guy who brings value into every room he walks into, not because he tries, but because it's just who he is.

Rhamen has been a friend that reminds me of the power of connection—the kind of friend who challenges you, supports you, and always tells it to you straight. He's someone I trust with both the highs and lows. And in this journey beyond the game, those kinds of friendships are worth their weight in gold.

He's part of my story now, just like all the teammates, coaches, mentors, and players who helped shape it. And as I look back, I realize that while basketball gave me unforgettable moments, it's the relationships I've built along the way that have truly made this journey worthwhile.

ACKNOWLEDGMENTS

"In the end, all that matters is the love you gave, the lives you touched, and the friends and family who stood by your side."
UNKNOWN

First and foremost, I want to say this: I know I'm going to accidentally leave some people out of this section. Please know that it's not intentional. There have been so many individuals—family, friends, mentors, teammates, coaches, and supporters—who have played a part in this journey. Each one has left a mark on my life, and I am truly grateful.

That said, I do want to give a special thanks to the following…

Most importantly, I want to thank God. None of this—this life, this journey, this story—would be possible without His grace, mercy, and perfect timing. His hand has guided me through every chapter of my life, even when I didn't always see it clearly in the moment.

To my loving wife, Erin—there aren't enough words to express what your support has meant to me throughout this journey. Thank you for standing beside me as I chased this next dream. Your unwavering belief in me never wavered—not once—and that quiet strength has been one of the greatest gifts in my life. Through every late night when I wrestled with the right words and every early morning when I questioned if this book would ever come together, you were there. You've been the steady foundation behind everything I've built. This book wouldn't exist without your love, your understanding, and your constant reminder that I was capable—even when I wasn't sure myself.

To my mom and dad, Nona and George—you taught me the value

ROOT

of hard work, humility, and heart. You believed in me before I ever believed in myself, and your sacrifices are the reason I ever had the chance to chase something bigger.

To my brother and sister, George and Natalie—you've been more than siblings. You've been my first teammates, my fiercest defenders, and my lifelong friends. I'm so proud to walk this life with you.

To my Uncle Ned Plunk—thank you for always being in my corner and showing up to every game. Your steady presence and constant encouragement have meant more to me than you probably know.

To my hometown crew—Bubba Hoover, Matt Hoover, Rob Bullington, Lamont Robinson, Russ Kennamore, Doug Rogers, and J.T. Livezey—thank you for being the other brothers that helped mold me. Y'all shaped me, pushed me, laughed with me, and carried me when I needed it most. I hope this book makes you proud.

To all of my teammates from Jr. Pro, junior high, and high school. Every practice, chocolate bus ride, win, and loss we shared helped shape me—not just as a player, but as a person. I'm grateful for the memories, the lessons, and the lifelong bonds we built along the way. I wouldn't trade those years for anything.

To all my Memphis teammates—thank you for the memories, the battles, and the brotherhood. A special shoutout to Earl Barron, Courtney Trask, Duane "Red" Erwin, Anthony Rice, and Jeremy Hunt—you each left your mark on my life in ways I'll always carry. What we shared in that locker room and on that court was real.

To the friends I have met along the way and who I consider brothers and sisters also—Gaylon Moore, John "J White" White, Rhamen Love-Lane, Steve Poindexter, Enelio Moreno, David Mason, B.J. Buford, Rodney Robinson, Nafeesa Farrakhan, Blake Allen, and Tamika "Red" Rogers—thank you for your presence, your laughter, and your loyalty. You each have brought light into my life in different ways.

To all of my Memphis coaches—thank you for challenging me, shaping me, and giving me the chance to grow. I'll never forget the lessons I learned under your leadership.

ACKNOWLEDGMENTS

To Coach Calipari—thank you for setting the standard, raising the bar, and helping me understand what it means to earn something every single day. You showed me what excellence looks like up close, and it changed me forever.

I want to thank my mother and father-in-law, Billy and Denise Brown, for their continued love and support. Your encouragement has meant so much to me over the years, and I'm truly grateful for the way you've stood by me and believed in me. Thank you for being such a steady presence in my life.

A special thank you to Steve Beavers. Without your help, this book would still be a scattered collection of thoughts and memories. You helped bring it to life, and I am deeply grateful.

And last but certainly not least...

To the incredible fans of Memphis:

Thank you. From the bottom of my heart—thank you.

You welcomed me, believed in me, and cheered for me long before you really knew me. Memphis isn't just a city—it's a heartbeat. It's passion, pride, grit, and loyalty wrapped into one unforgettable place. And being able to wear "Memphis" across my chest and represent this city will always be one of the greatest honors of my life.

Whether you were in the stands at the Pyramid, watching from home, or stopping me on the street with a word of encouragement, you made me feel like I belonged. Your support fueled me through every early morning workout, every late-night bus ride, every challenge, and every celebration.

Memphis fans are different. You love hard. You expect greatness. And you never forget your own. That's what makes this place so special—and why I'll always be proud to say I was a Memphis Tiger.

Thank you for letting me be part of your story.

ABOUT THE AUTHOR

Nathaniel Root is a former University of Memphis basketball player whose journey from a small-town walk-on to a Division I scholarship athlete captured the hearts of a city. Raised in McNairy County, Tennessee, Root's story is one of resilience, grit, and unshakable belief. Off the court, he serves as the Vice President of Partner Relations and Executive Director of The Root Agency, where he leads efforts to help nonprofits raise funds. He is also a mentor, motivational speaker, and passionate advocate for youth development in basketball, using his platform to inspire the next generation to chase their dreams with relentless determination. *Root: A Memphis Hoops Dream* is his debut memoir—a tribute to faith, family, friends, and the power of perseverance.

To contact Root for speaking engagements/appearances or follow him on social media:

www.facebook.com/root32
www.instagram.com/theteamroot/
www.tiktok.com/@theteamroot?lang=en
www.theteamroot.com

www.ingramcontent.com/pod-product-compliance
Lightning Source LLC
Chambersburg PA
CBHW050251010526
44107CB00003B/277